WHAT
HAPPENS IN
PUBLIC
RELATIONS

WHAT HAPPENS IN PUBLIC RELATIONS

Gerald J. Voros & Paul H. Alvarez,
Editors

A Division of
AMERICAN MANAGEMENT ASSOCIATIONS

ACKNOWLEDGMENTS

WE WISH TO EXPRESS our appreciation to the following who contributed to the writing of this book: Robert J. Aiello, Edwin F. Brennan, Richard H. Conner, David R. Drobis, Jacob L. Engle, William H. Friedman, Larry Jenkins, John M. Maddigan, Jr., Jack Murphy, Stephen D. Pisinski, Guy C. Read, James J. Roop, Betty Saneholtz, Robert Schulin, Gene L. Slaughter, Thomas L. Taylor, and Linda Taber. All are present or former professional staff members of Ketchum MacLeod & Grove Public Relations, Botsford Ketchum Public Relations, or Carol Moberg Communications.

Library of Congress Cataloging in Publication Data

Main entry under title:

What happens in public relations.

   Includes index.
   1. Public relations. I. Voros, Gerald J.
II. Alvarez, Paul H.
HM263.W445   659.2   80-69700
ISBN 0-8144-5652-9

FIRST PRINTING

PREFACE

THIS BOOK is about public relations. It's written for managers, not for students or beginners. As such, it is more about how to manage public relations than how to do it. Naturally, a knowledge of effective techniques is helpful—indeed sometimes necessary—to manage them, and so we have cited examples to explain these techniques. We also see the book as a reference tool, helping to guide the manager in new areas as he encounters them.

As we developed the book, we had two kinds of readers in mind: the upwardly mobile public relations professional who is assuming new responsibilities for communications outside his existing areas of expertise, and the corporate executive who has been given overall management responsibility for public relations but whose experience has been in other disciplines. There are many of both.

One-fourth of the 35,000 to 40,000 public relations professionals in the United States change jobs each year, according to *Public Relations Journal,* not including those who assume new responsibilities in an upward or lateral move within their own organization.

Increasingly, a new layer of executives is being charged with managing the public relations function according to a 1978 survey of the nation's top 100 manufacturing companies by Jack O'Dwyer's *Newsletter.* O'Dwyer stated this layer includes such titles as VP–Administration, VP–Constituency Relations, VP–Planning and Administration, and Senior VP–Corporate Services Staff. The background of these executives is typically outside communications. This is true of chief executive officers who continue to supervise one half of all public relations departments that were surveyed in O'Dwyer's *Directory of Corporate Communications.*

This book stems from the realization that more and more executives who have the ultimate responsibility for public relations do not have experience in it. Consequently, most of them have little practical knowledge with which to judge the effectiveness of existing communications efforts. They also do not know what to expect from the function in new efforts.

To help establish that base, we have provided an overview of what can be accomplished in the various specialized areas of public relations. Experts have contributed chapters on subjects in which they specialize, often citing parallel public relations situations that can be applied from one specialty to another.

In writing the book, we have assumed some basic knowledge of public relations practice, tools, and theory—if not through experience, then through observation. The book fills the need for a document that will broaden the knowledge of the public relations professional and enable management to better understand—and manage—the day-to-day working of the function.

Existing literature does not meet this need. Most of it is concentrated in three main areas: (1) basic college textbooks; (2) esoteric discussions of social and economic factors affecting the practice of public relations; and (3) specialized books devoted to individual public relations tools.

We have aimed, instead, to blend theory and practice into a working tool for career public relations professionals and a guide to managing the public relations function. Although this effort represents many hours of work by public relations professionals whose cumulative experience totals several hundred years, we do not claim to supply all the answers. No professional—or group of professionals—can do this. Public opinion changes daily. The public relations professional who is trying to influence that opinion must constantly monitor effectiveness of tactics and be prepared to change them as the needs and perceptions of the public change.

The first step in effectively managing public relations is to recognize the fluidity of the public relations environment and to follow the basic four-step public relations process of research, programming, execution, and evaluation.

The manager who wants to gauge the effectiveness of these steps needs a reference point. We hope this book provides it.

THE EDITORS

CONTENTS

1: Research and Communications Audits

THE CORNERSTONE of good public relations is research. This is not one man's opinion. The Public Relations Society of America identifies it as the first step in the four-step public relations method for professional development. The other steps are planning, execution, and evaluation.

Whether you are reacting to an obvious problem or merely trying to determine if a problem really exists, research provides an accurate guide. Needs and economics do not change—they affect both corporate PR people and members of counseling firms. For any professional, conducting a public relations effort without proper research can waste money or, worse, can result in failure.

Even though the budget may be limited, some effort should be made to determine the attitudes and opinions of the audiences you are trying to reach. Ideally, a formal research study should be made. It can be a structured questionnaire, a combination questionnaire and interview approach, or, preferably, a sophisticated in-depth study conducted among 10 percent of your audience. If none of these methods is feasible because of time pressure or lack of funds, it is advisable to conduct a few telephone interviews with people in organizations that have substantial influence in the industry or area in which you expect to concentrate your public relations effort.

Communicators who assume that they understand a situation and act on erroneous assumptions can be in for a rude awakening. Many things are not what they seem to be, and research can pinpoint specific targets that can be aimed at by public relations programs. The amount of time and money spent on research depends on the complexity and/or importance of the problem, as perceived by the

1

public relations practitioner. However, the research needed is often already available and no new large-scale, expensive surveys need to be commissioned. If there is a problem in marketing a product, it is likely that consumer companies and industrial companies have already done initial market studies. These studies should be surveyed to determine if they fill the need of the public relations person and, if not, what inadequacies exist. For example, some studies provide information about a market, but not about media perceptions. This can be corrected by contacts with the media to find out what they want to know about the product or service being developed, and why they want to know it. Such a review of existing research data, combined with off-the-cuff personal study, might indicate that several approaches would work. In that case, a test of the feasibility of one approach over another should be undertaken.

One form of public relations research is the communications audit. It can be done by public relations professionals, either those on staff or those with a public relations agency. The audit examines the perceptions of media, management, and employees. In a paper written by Gerald C. Wollan and Donald G. Padilla for the Counselors Monograph Series (issued by the Counselors Section of the Public Relations Society of America), the public relations audit is discussed in some detail. The article lists key questions for which public relations professionals seek answers in an audit procedure:

1. Does management want to find out something or prove something?
2. What does management want from a proper audit?
3. How does the management wish the organization to be perceived?
4. How does management think the organization currently is perceived?
5. What is the scope of the audit?
6. What is the role of the organization's public relations function?
7. How and with what effect has the public relations function been carried out?

At least nine areas of public relations practice falter if not based on research—employee communications, industrial relations, consumer public relations, financial public relations, community relations, government relations, consumer affairs, event publicity, and corporate advertising. These are discussed below.

The effectiveness of *employee communications* can be enhanced through the use of attitude studies and communications surveys. Determining the attitudes of employees about such subjects as wages, benefits, working conditions, overtime, corporate profits, and product quality is important. Any employee communications specialist can attest to the importance of knowing what sort of attitudes his readers or listeners have before he begins to be able to talk with them in an understanding manner.

Once the attitudes are determined, the communications study aims at determining the methods of communications that are best for the employee and how they can be best utilized. Personal interviews, telephone surveys, and do-it-yourself questionnaires can be used in combination or individually to obtain this information.

Industrial relations is not the same as employee communications, although they impact on each other. Bringing about an understanding of the union contract, developing reasonable demand proposals at negotiation time, developing programs for union avoidance, and presenting management's views during crises such as when strikes are threatened depend on having good information to work with. The information is accumulated through the use of short-term audits similar to those for employee communications.

Consumer public relations emphasizes marketing information that may or may not be used exclusively for the public relations function. In addition, a survey of media to determine acceptability of messages, demonstrations, and spokespeople is often conducted by telephone interviews and by personal interviews in editors' and news directors' offices.

Financial public relations, which may or may not be part of an investor relations program, has played a pioneering role in demonstrating to many executive officers the value of research. Penetrating interviews with leading analysts have brought to light their views of the strengths or weaknesses of the company being studied, and provide the keys to identifying the messages that should be addressed to the analyst and the investor. For example, if management strength is questioned, then current or future managers should be presented to analysts through meetings. If lawsuits have adversely affected interest in a company or if expensive pollution control equipment impacts negatively on earnings and has led to a loss of favor among analysts, these questions can be addressed in annual reports, quarterly reports, and special reports to the financial community.

Community relations is an area in which management is usually willing to allow the community's opinion to guide a public relations program. If a new plant is to be constructed, the public relations manager should know well ahead of time what the attitudes of residents and elected public officials are. Too often, studies are not made until a proposal is blocked by court action taken by a group of citizens or by one official. At that time, it is too late for such a study to positively affect community relations.

Determining attitudes is an important part of community relations research because the media are the means for carrying the messages to a community. It is no great revelation that a hostile newspaper can defeat many community relations programs.

Government relations research can be highly structured or it can be a daily monitoring of activities in government. Many corporations maintain "monitoring activities" in Washington, D.C., and at state capitals in an effort to have early knowledge of activities that may help or hurt the corporation. Such research generally consists of maintaining regular personal contacts and reading government publications and releases. Research should not be confused with lobbying. Lobbyists can use research information, and frequently research is done by registered lobbyists, but research is only one step in the government affairs program.

Consumer affairs differs from consumer public relations in that the research is directed at an analysis of consumer complaints in order to determine how to better talk to the consumer. Many times, companies find that much of the research on consumer attitudes has already been done by the government, by associations, or by consumer groups themselves. In that case, their research effort can become a study of existing studies.

Event publicity is something many public relations practitioners ignore when the subject of research is discussed. It should not be. Generally, events are staged as a means of calling attention to a product, an anniversary, or a new facility. Judging whether the event will accomplish what management hopes to achieve should not be left to intuition. Large-scale events are expensive, and the company's chances of getting its money's worth can be increased by conducting research among target audiences in advance. This should include attitudinal research as well as research on acceptability by the target audience.

Corporate advertising is an area in which research is readily accepted, partly because of the large amounts of money involved and partly because the media have already conducted research in an effort to sell advertising time or space. In order to be certain that the message management wants to deliver is being received, ads and concepts are often pre-tested. Including offers for annual reports or position papers in an ad is one way of measuring response to a corporate advertising campaign.

Greater use of research to measure public relations performance is needed. Many factors are creating change within the public relations field today. Social issues, economics, geopolitics, multinational business, and the growing sophistication of public relations professionals have exerted increased pressures to measure performance of the activities planned and implemented by public relations specialists. The need for performance acceptability has two facets: (1) a growing need to know exactly what the public relations activities contribute to the organization's effort to communicate and (2) an increasing desire to learn which activities produce the best results.

Feedback is needed from the public to assist in the planning, refinement, and implementation of present and future public relations programs. Scores of case histories attest to the fallacies of shotgun PR. One example is a classic case in which a large corporation budgeted more than $1 million for sound-muffling equipment at one of its major plants solely on the basis of a great number of phone complaints that were received daily in the late afternoon.

The first inclination of the management and the public relations people was to install the muffling equipment, concurrent with timely publicity and advertising to assure residents of the area that "the company cares and is doing something about the problem." Fortunately, the advice of public relations counsel was sought before any action was taken. Counsel was skeptical. The complaints appeared to arrive almost on schedule, shortly before closing time. Few of the calls came while the equipment causing the noise was at peak operation. Moreover, most of those who called did not identify themselves.

With these facts at hand, counsel suggested to the client that some effort be made to determine not only the source of the calls but the geographical location of the people who made them. This was accomplished through a unique research approach worked out with the industrial development division of the local chamber of commerce. The study was formally sponsored by the industrial development group.

Using a map of the area surrounding the plant, researchers drew circles at intervals ranging from a quarter of a mile to two miles from the factory. A random sample was selected from each of these areas and personal interviews were conducted at the respondents' homes. Interviewers introduced themselves as representatives of a research organization that had been retained by the chamber of commerce to determine attitudes and opinions about the progress and effect of industrial development in the area.

More than 100 residents were interviewed with very positive results. The question of noise and pollution was adroitly worked into each interview. The few complaints about noise were confined to the area immediately surrounding the plant. But there was no consensus, even among this group, that the noise they were concerned about really constituted a problem. The interviews revealed, however, that a real estate developer who had purchased property within sight of the plant was the instigator of the phone complaints.

Naturally, this information completely changed the company's attitude about the situation. Routine public relations procedures were resumed after management representatives met with the real estate developer and offered to take much less expensive measures to reduce the noise level in the immediate vicinity of the plant.

Another situation involving community relations for a major corporation developed in its largest plant community because sales of one of the company's popular consumer products were far less than those of a major competitor. The problem surfaced dramatically when executives of the company discovered that their favorite department store did not stock the product. The problem appeared to be one of inadequate distribution and promotion. But communications people were brought into the picture because company officials were highly sensitive about poor identity for their consumer goods in a city where the company's payroll and purchases were major economic factors.

Depth interviews were conducted among a large sample of business, civic, and educational leaders. Much to the dismay of the client, the study showed that few of the opinion leaders identified the consumer products with the company. They viewed the company only as a large important industrial corporation that contributed substantially to the economic growth of the community.

In addition to recommending expansion of promotion and distribution of the consumer item, the survey report also urged a special campaign among the company's industrial workers to better identify and promote the firm's consumer products. Special inserts were prepared for the employee publication, and discount sales to employees were held in all the plants.

We have just seen two cases where attitude and opinion research helped companies redefine problems and develop more appropriate public relations activities. The following sections discuss some other ways such research can be useful in PR programming.

Trade Media Relations

A large industrial public relations firm, many of whose clients relied on product case histories as an important marketing tool, saw a steady increase in budgets for case history preparation and placement. The agency became concerned that the trade media might not be able to absorb such substantial increases in case history volume.

To protect the client's budgets and its own reputation for distributing high-quality trade news, the firm surveyed 103 trade magazine editors in 27 specialized fields of interest. Seventy-six editors responded, a return of 74 percent. Of these, 80 percent said their interest was unchanged; they used case histories and planned to continue doing so. Twenty percent indicated their interest had increased.

This research enabled the agency to continue to recommend and substantiate the use of case histories as productive PR communications.

Broadcast Publicity Opportunities

Placement of spokespersons on broadcast media can be expensive and often frustrating.

Research is an effective way to avoid these pitfalls. A recent in-depth study was made among consumer reporters of television stations affiliated with the three major networks in the top 75 markets. Radio affiliates were surveyed in the top 30 markets. In addition to the in-depth study, questionnaires were sent to 225 television and 90 radio stations.

All the consumer reporters questioned were interested in featuring a spokesperson whose subject is unique, timely, and relevant to their audience. Nearly all the reporters believed a commercial product reference is often necessary when discussing the industry in general, in order to differentiate and emphasize the advantages and disadvantages of a product. Respondents unanimously voiced their disapproval of blatant commercial "plugs" and "sell tactics" by spokespersons for the sake of getting their product mentioned on the air.

Around 90 percent of consumer reporters surveyed indicated a willingness to evaluate unsolicited subject material for interviews. Respondents were interested in filling their programming needs with material from outside sources such as wire services, consumer reports, private industry, associations, companies, and corporations. In general, respondents said they prefer to receive background information on the person to be interviewed at least three weeks in advance of the requested air date and appreciate a follow-up phone call a week later to confirm the interview. They also indicated that they like material involving fast-breaking headline news to be phoned in immediately, with the names and phone numbers of appropriate contacts who can act as spokespersons.

For almost any area of public relations, there is a vast body of research readily available from business, college, and general libraries. Other research is available from public relations agencies, which conduct research on a variety of subjects ranging from employee communications to publication and television station interests.

The Foundation for Public Relations Research and Education helps develop the skills and enhance the professionalism of public relations practitioners. More than 100 research proposals have been approved by the Foundation. It can be contacted at Suite 1006, 575 Madison Avenue, New York, N.Y. 10022.

Film producers, mat services, and news distribution organizations will conduct contributing studies and can provide insight into specific problems concerning the quality of communications and how it can be improved.

The Professional's Guide to Public Relations Services, published by Richard Weiner, Inc., 888 Seventh Avenue, New York, N.Y. 10019, is regularly updated and contains a chapter on research that provides a list and brief description of research materials and services available to the public relations person. It also contains information on specialized newsletters that report on social science research related to practical public relations.

Marketing research companies are listed in the "Green Book" published by the New York chapter of the American Marketing Association, 60 E. 42nd Street, New York, N.Y. 10017.

To find out what kind of programs have been successful, examine the programs that have won the Silver Anvil award competition, conducted by the Public Relations Society of America. These are available from the national headquarters, 845 Third Avenue, New York, N.Y. 10022.

2: Preparing a Public Relations Program

Through the Looking Glass

"Cheshire-puss," she began rather timidly, "would you tell me which way I ought to go from here?"

"That depends a good deal on where you want to get to," said the cat.

"I don't much care where . . ." said Alice.

"Then it doesn't matter which way you go," said the cat.

That whimsical meeting between Alice and the Cheshire Cat in Lewis Carroll's *Alice's Adventures in Wonderland* describes the situation in which public relations people may find themselves—unless, of course, they put some sound thinking and planning into their public relations activities.

Here are a few facts that must be considered:

- Every institution—public and private—is facing intense competition in the marketplace for ideas, services, and products. For example, consumer goods marketers must find a solution to skyrocketing advertising costs and advertising clutter.
- The growing threat of takeovers is causing many sleepless nights for many chief executive officers.
- Changes in the financial market are putting great burdens on companies that want to reach investment and lending institutions.
- Management must deal with a younger, better educated, more sophisticated workforce that has far different personal expectations from those of earlier generations.

11

Surveys are revealing problems that are even more basic and disturbing. Institutions are operating under the microscopic eye of a public that is exhibiting a growing distrust of them. Furthermore, the public has discovered how to use its muscle to change things. Pressure by consumerists, environmentalists, civil rights groups, employees, and others has created an environment in which a public relations problem can mean more than a potential loss of "good-will." It can seriously threaten an institution's ability to survive. The great attention that chief executive officers are directing to the public relations function indicates the importance top management places on these problems.

A January 1979 survey by *PR Reporter,* a weekly newsletter for the profession published in Exeter, New Hampshire, shows that more than 88 percent of the chief executive officers queried now meet with outside groups. Nearly 85 percent engage in public speaking, almost half lobby on behalf of their organizations, and two-thirds are involved in press conferences and media contacts. A third of the CEOs make radio and television appearances.

Public relations is solidifying its position as a management tool for problem solving. Although this can be a heady trend for public relations people, it is not without pitfalls. As public relations moves into the management hierarchy, top management is demanding the same disciplines and performance evaluations as it does from any other management function. Management wants assurances that the work is clearly meeting the needs of the organization that is paying for it.

Are You Doing the Right Things?

Public relations people are being asked less frequently "Are you doing things right?" The ability to write press releases or edit a house organ is taken for granted. The question now being asked is, "Are you doing the right things?"

Consider the consternation of the public relations person who has feverishly filled volumes of clip books on the fruits of his activity only to have the CEO demand, "Show me how all this has helped!"

The demand cannot be answered by attempting to explain the value of an article in *The New York Times* or that public relations is less a science than an art and therefore can't be measured. The answer lies in proper planning and programming. To do that, the public relations professional must look at his function from management's perspective.

Who Are Those Guys and What Do They Want?

The top executives of most institutions have come up from the ranks of engineering, production, marketing, law, or finance. They have been trained to think in black-and-white terms. Until lately, many have perceived little reason to obtain sufficient insight into the communications process to understand what can and cannot be expected from public relations.

Public relations has been something of a gray function. Many practitioners still feel that what they are doing is intuitive in nature and must be accepted more or less on faith or because it seems logical. Often activities that the practitioner sees as helpful may be viewed by management as very narrow or not germane to its objectives.

This situation need not exist.

A properly conceived public relations plan can do much to bridge the gap between management and the PR professional. It can force the public relations person to think in terms of management's objectives and can help management understand the function's potential. Such a plan can provide an opportunity for mutual education.

Some public relations people argue that attempting such a plan can place the function in a box from which there is no escape. Successful managements learn to adjust to changes. They understand from experience that plans change as circumstances change. The main concern of management is that public relations activities are relevant to the objectives of the organization and that the function is managing events, so far as is humanly possible, and not letting events manage it. Management does not want to spend time and money on peripheral activities that mean little in the total scheme. It does not want surprises. That means PR people must have solid reasons to change directions and must convince management that the changes are necessary.

SET YOUR GOALS

A public relations program starts with a clear understanding of the goals of the management. Public relations goals should not be confused with management's goals. It is doubtful, for example, that the goals of an organization include more effective communication with employees. In a business organization, management's goals may be more like these:

Increase share of market for product X.
Introduce three new consumer products to the marketplace.
Broaden the shareholder base of the company.
Increase plant production by x percent.
Seek acquisition to complement present product line.

In a nonprofit organization, they may be:

Reduce organization's dependence on government grants.
Increase government grants.
Expand services in area Y.

The list could go on and on. The challenge is to know the goals and relate PR activities to those objectives that will help the organization.

START AT THE BEGINNING

The key to an effective public relations program is to organize the components into a complete, logical, and persuasive document. A public relations plan should tell a story. It should present the procedures that will help meet certain objectives and explain how their progress will be measured.

Some of the most successful public relations planners say they try to envision a doctor–patient relationship. A patient wants to know what the situation is and what the doctor intends to do about it. He doesn't want medical terminology. He doesn't want a discourse in human anatomy. He wants the facts in understandable terms.

Top management feels the same way. The CEO does not have time to wade through irrelevant material. He doesn't want to be preached to. The plan should simply tell the facts, completely and concisely, and state the specific public relations solutions.

Remember that public relations is only one of many potentially conflicting considerations that management must reconcile. Nevertheless, once a decision is made, management expects things to move ahead rapidly. The program should place the public relations organization in a position to do that.

Think How, *Not* What

The tendency of many practitioners is to leap directly into audiences or techniques without thinking about their place or role. The first step should be to determine these organizational goals that public relations can affect and the public relations objectives to help meet them.

For example, a food company may desire a bigger share of the market for a product that consumerists perceive as "not nutritious." A public relations objective might be to explain the nutritional value of the product.

Who's Out There?

Once the objectives are delineated, the audiences, or "publics," that can help the organization achieve its goals should be defined. Each public is a group of people with common interests. The error is to define each one too broadly, as employees, shareholders, or customers—this is, as a group without further delineation.

The customers for a food product may be women. But what age

group? What educational level? What income? What interests? Are there distribution problems that will limit a message to certain geographical areas?

Similar questions must be asked about employees. Supervisory people have different personal goals and perceptions about an organization than do clerical and technical employees. Women have different perceptions and needs than men. Younger employees differ significantly from older ones.

The obvious need for this information has sparked a long overdue interest in polls, surveys, and audits that measure opinion. Public relations people are finding these tools are valuable, not only from a planning viewpoint, but also for feedback and evaluation of the ongoing program.

Any effective public relations program, in our opinion, must carefully segment the publics to be reached. This is necessary to determine what opinions will have to be changed or reinforced to achieve the objectives.

This kind of fact finding can be surprising to management as well as to the public relations person. A key audience may be so apathetic to an issue that it may be very difficult to get those people to even think about the issue, much less to act on it. An approach to this public would be entirely different from one to an activist group.

Research can help decide which messages will work and where they will work best. That essentially is the core job of public relations. Effective public relations is getting through to people. No form of communication works unless people receive the message, understand the content, and are motivated to act on it.

FRAME THE PLAN IN YOUR MIND

A good plan must be cohesive. It is useless to outline a statement of objectives and audiences and follow this with seemingly disassociated activities, each working independently, each giving out its own message. The frame of a plan should analyze management's objectives and audiences; delineate the environment that is impacting on these objectives and how it affects them; and outline the overall thrust of the program and what management can expect of the activities to be undertaken.

The frame gives the techniques meaning. Properly presented, it translates the activities into a campaign that will result in an overall solution to the problems management faces.

THINK ABOUT TECHNIQUES

Techniques should reflect the interests of management. Management is not interested in simply spending more money, but it can be persuaded to do that if it feels it is spending money effectively. Don't assume management is familiar with feature stories, television film strips, and other techniques or with their value or why they are being used. Such assumptions are usually wrong.

The Technique Is the Vehicle

Techniques are vehicles for communication, not the solution to the problem. In determining a technique, think about its role.

As communications vehicles, techniques should relate to a particular audience and the delivery of a particular message. Radio scripts, television films, and special events, for example, should be coordinated so that each is hitting the target it is best equipped to hit and each is sending the message it is best equipped to deliver. That does not mean that each is delivering a different message. Two or three ideas are about as many as a public will remember in any one year unless it knows the organization well. However, a limited number of ideas can be expressed in several ways—each designed to appeal to a particular medium.

One approach to this is to think up specific headlines to illustrate the message that is to be delivered. For example, one of management's objectives may be to capture a percentage of the highly competitive air conditioning market with a new product. A public relations objective might be to help this goal by positioning the organization's capabilities among key buying influences and, if needed, the financial community. Sample headlines might be: for the trade and business press, "XYZ Company, A Hot Competitor in the Cold War"; for the consumer press, "How to Centrally Condition Your Older Home without Spending a Bundle"; for the local newspapers, "How XYZ's Entry into the Cold War Means More Jobs."

NOW IT'S TIME TO WRITE

The most effective plan uses a simple format. It starts with the frame, which consists of a background section, a statement of the objectives, a delineation by segment of the audiences to be reached, and a section presenting the overall strategy to be used and the reasons. The frame is followed by a section on the techniques and the reasons supporting each recommendation. Next comes a timetable for implementation, a section on evaluating the progress, and finally, costs. If exhibits are attached, they are referred to by number in the text.

Let's examine each of the components.

Why Should Management Care?

Start with a statement of the purpose of the plan. This can be done with a few clear, concise sentences about the problems that are being addressed.

The background section should review some history. It can describe those events that make the problem serious enough to warrant attention and then outline the specific factors that concern management and their potential effect. This section need not be long. It should be complete but not too detailed. Resist the temptation to be carried away and write a book to explain the background of a problem. Be positive. Translate the problems into opportunities for management.

What Are You Trying to Do?

Be realistic in setting forth the public relations objectives. Do not promise management the moon and the stars. For example, do not state that you want to halt government pressure when research and common sense indicate the best that can be expected is to relieve it slightly.

If research reveals that a massive effort will be needed to accomplish an objective, consider whether the organization is really in a position to do something. Does it have the resources? Is there enough time? Is it really the kind of effort in which the organization should get involved? Is the risk of failure greater than the potential for success? It is better to do one thing effectively than to try to do many things.

Who and How?

Delineate the audiences for management, both by categories and subgroups. Outline the influence each has on a particular objective. Point out that reaching each audience will require a different method. Explain the most efficient way to do this and how to build the desired impression.

Putting It All Together

The part of the plan on implementing the program may not necessarily be the most important element in management's eyes. Experienced programmers suggest that, if the plan has been carefully constructed, selling the techniques is far less difficult.

Here are some general guidelines for writing techniques into a program:

1. Keep the written text as short as possible. Repetition may be a very real irritant to a CEO who must review the plan and who has little time and a full agenda.

2. Brevity does not take priority over completeness. Use exhibits to explain an idea wherever possible. Don't hesitate to relate ideas back to the audience and objectives. Some planners add

a review section that is designed to do this. It follows the detailed section on techniques and is simply an outline of what has proceeded.

3. Be sure that the message to be conveyed is appropriate to the medium, that the medium will give the message timely exposure, and that there are no negative consequences of using that medium. For example, a white paper issued by a company might be relevant for a key government group but not for the general public. National consumer publications work as much as six months in advance on material; that can be reason enough to consider other media. A story in a national magazine such as *Fortune* might be very desirable from management's perspective. Most of these publications, however, do their own research, so the company should be able to stand the scrutiny. In recommending a new employee publication, remember that it will compete for attention among all the other magazines and newspapers the employee reads. The same holds true for in-house television programs. The employee sees high-quality productions on his TV at home, so "talking heads" or messages flashed on a television screen at work won't generate interest simply because they are produced by the company.

What Happens When?

The timetable for implementation can be submitted in any form—a chart, a graph, or a month-by-month outline of what will be accomplished. This section is important because it shows management the activity level it should expect from the public relations function at a particular time. If changes in timing arise, the public relations manager can redefine what has happened and explain this effect on the timing of the program. In short, a timetable eliminates surprises.

The Matter of Evaluation

Accountability is one of the prime responsibilities of management. Public relations cannot really be considered part of management until it is willing to be accountable for the success or failure of its activities.

The results of a public relations effort can be ascertained in many ways. Some of the measurements we have experienced include complicated formulas that evaluate the quality of television time generated and the quality or quantity of mail generated, before and after awareness and opinion surveys, and studies of traffic generation and product movement.

A key to accountability is knowing the way management measures performance and then finding how this kind of measurement can be applied to public relations efforts. For instance, an investor relations manager may realize that his management closely watches Standard & Poor's and rates the company's performance in terms of both the 400 industrial averages and the averages of the company's own industry. As a result, he evaluates his activities by charting the improvement in the company's performance since he began his effort.

Obtaining advance agreement on the criteria for evaluation can be critical. If it is not done, a program can fail in management's eyes regardless of how successful it appears to the practitioner.

The Wrap-up

Not every plan has to have a conclusion. However, such a wrap-up has proved effective in dealing with a management that is instituting a public relations effort for the first time or that is wary because of past failures.

One effective technique is shown on the following page. It lists management objectives (in this case, by number) across the top and then shows how each major element of the program meets those objectives.

How Much Does It Cost?

In some organizations, the public relations program is developed to fit within a fixed amount of money. However, if public relations activities are truly designed to accomplish a mission, then the overall plan should come first and the budget last.

Most of our clients prefer a line approach to budgeting, which

Recommendations	Objectives										
	1	2	3	4	5	6	7	8	9	10	11
Public Service/Corporate											
Corporate Faculty	x	x	x	x	x	x	x	x	x	x	x
Discussion Outline	x	x	x	x		x					x
Media Tour	x	x	x	x	x	x	x	x	x	x	x
National Media Contact	x	x	x	x	x	x	x	x	x	x	x
Local Releases	x	x	x	x	x	x	x	x	x	x	x
Task Force	x		x	x	x	x	x				x
White Papers	x		x	x	x	x	x			x	x
Research	x		x			x	x				x
Evaluation	x		x			x	x				x
Financial											
Research	x					x			x	x	
Regional Money Centers	x	x					x	x	x	x	
Financial Literature	x	x	x		x	x	x		x	x	
Shareholder Relations	x	x			x	x	x	x	x	x	
Media Relations	x	x	x	x		x	x	x	x	x	
Employee Communications											
Employee Attitude Study	x					x		x			x
Special Presentations	x					x	x	x			x
Employee Recognition Program	x					x	x	x	x		x
Employee Publications	x					x		x			x
Follow-up Survey	x					x	x	x			x
Community Relations											
Community Participation Audit	x	x	x		x	x	x	x			x
Community Recognition Program	x	x	x	x	x	x	x				x
Community Leader Mailings	x	x	x	x	x	x	x				x

assigns a cost to each activity. This offers one advantage: If the program must be reduced, it is easy to determine where to do so and to assess the effect of the overall program.

Too few people prepare a budget with realistic figures. They are usually too low in their estimates, because they do not take the time to go to sources to determine costs before they commit them to paper. Estimated costs are often based on past experience, and that's being unrealistic in an inflationary economy.

Another failing is to determine budgets only on the basis of staff salaries and production costs, not including overhead items such as employee benefits. Other budget items to consider are fees for temporary help, recruitment expenses if staff is to be expanded, moving expenses, costs for employee training and professional development, travel and entertainment expenses, professional dues and subscription prices, contributions, duplication expenses, costs of supplies and postage, allocations for salary increases of present staff, fees for agency services, and such indirect expenses as allowances for equipment, light, and heat.

Budgeting is as much a fine art as is programming. Attention to detail early can save embarrassment later.

3: The Fine Art
of Budgeting

BUDGETING is a bugaboo for many public relations managers. They don't understand it and don't want to become involved with it.

"Let the accountants handle the budgets" is a familiar cry among those public relations practitioners who, having served perhaps as publication editors or media relations experts, are promoted to public relations manager or director and are greeted by computer printouts and columns of figures.

Neither the accountants nor anyone else should plan budgets for you. By turning over budget responsibility to someone else, you lose a great deal of power and management influence. Conversely, becoming adept at budgeting will allow you to become part of the management team and strengthen the public relations function within your organization.

As a public relations manager, you must take charge of budgeting, because management demands that public relations budgets, as with all other functions, be integrated into an organization's overall objectives and expenditures. The approach to budgeting may reflect the organization's attitude to the public relations function. The public relations budget should warrant the attention of top management. It should not be the first place to cut costs.

In today's climate of management by objectives, zero-base financial planning, and scrutiny of public relations for its return on investment, budgeting has become a fine art. This chapter, then, is designed to help you get control of budgeting so that you can approach the flowcharts without trepidation and create your own work of art. The first part of the chapter discusses planning the budget for internal functions, whatever they may be, and the second part deals with managing the budgets of outside counsel.

BUDGETING FOR THE INTERNAL FUNCTION

The functions, and hence the budgets, of public relations departments vary among organizations. Because of the diverse nature of organizations, this part of the chapter will not attempt to set forth an exact formula for preparing a public relations budget but rather will offer general guidelines that will be useful in arriving at a budget regardless of the individual needs of an organization.

Management Budgeting Methods

Management may use several budgeting methods in determining how much money should be spent on public relations.

Some companies, particularly manufacturers of consumer packaged goods, may use a percent-of-sales basis to determine funds for all promotional activities, including public relations. This is fine if all public relations activities are used to directly promote a company's products, but it does not incorporate the costs of other endeavors such as producing an annual report.

Another approach in establishing budget amounts may be a percent-of-advertising. This practice, however, relegates public relations to an adjunct of advertising and makes it difficult to budget public relations activities on their own merits, especially if the activities are not directly related to advertising. It is even more confining to product promotion than the percent-of-sales method.

The most enlightened, and fortunately most prevalent, practice is the one that rates public relations as a corporate management function and considers all public relations areas of involvement—product publicity, employee communications, investor relations—in determining a public relations budget. Consequently, public relations is not identified with a product or promotional campaign but as part of the total communications effort.

Using this approach, top management usually has a general idea, based on operating income or profit, of how much it can afford to spend on public relations compared with other corporate functions to meet the organization's needs and objectives. This means a public relations budget is based on the public relations contribution to the organization. Unlike fixed-percentage methods, this approach supplies the flexibility that is needed by a public relations manager to tackle a particularly troublesome problem, break new ground, or respond to a growing need. If this method is used, a public relations manager generally will have the most flexibility and responsibility in determining how the public relations budget is going to be spent.

In many large corporations, public relations is regarded not only as a corporate function but also as part of the "service package"— along with the legal and accounting functions—that aids the corporation's various companies, divisions, or departments. If a corporate public relations office spends a great deal of time helping to promote one division's products, the cost of such help is usually charged to that division as part of its operating expenses. Such corporate-wide activities as annual reports and employee publications usually are regarded as part of the corporation's public relations cost. These costs may or may not, depending upon organizational structure and accounting procedures, be charged against individual companies or divisions as part of general corporate overhead.

Some might believe that this cost accounting method unduly emphasizes the public relations function as a cost center, but public relations managers should not be disturbed by this. If they are skilled in their profession, they will be able to show how public relations—just as the accounting and legal departments—makes a significant contribution to the corporation's survival and growth.

Preparing the Budget

The essential steps in preparing a public relations budget are (1) have a plan; (2) learn the organization's budgeting system; (3) put the figures into a usable form; (4) monitor spending; and (5) measure and report results in relation to expenditures.

HAVE A PLAN

In preparing a budget, it is essential to have a detailed public relations program that contains objectives and the specific activities planned to meet those objectives. Obviously, there is some interplay between plan and budget. In costing out the program, certain planned activities may prove too costly and will be reduced in scope or eliminated. On the other hand, additional funds may be required to implement those projects that are necessary to achieve the objectives. Previous programs and budgets probably can serve as starting points and guidelines if no dramatic revision of the public relations function has occurred or is contemplated.

One of the most important aspects of program planning and budgeting is to develop a program timetable indicating the schedule of the year's major projects. An example is shown in Exhibit 1.

Such a timetable will serve as a guide not only to work load but also to expenditures. For example, if the financial communications portion of your program calls for the annual report to be published in April, obviously there will be extensive activity and expenditures in this area during the first four months of the year. Processing of supplier invoices will require an additional month.

As you will read later, a program timetable will be useful in monitoring your expenditures.

LEARN THE SYSTEM

The next step in preparing a budget is to know the budgeting system for the organization and how it applies to the public relations function. Public relations must compete for funds with other management functions, so knowing the budgeting system at least insures a place at the start of the race.

Know the formal stages of preparing and submitting a budget. When should you begin planning? Whom should you consult in the process? Are there specific forms and styles to use? When is your first budget recommendation due? Who reviews your recommendation?

You should know who approves your budget. Is it a budget committee or an individual? Is it the chief executive officer, or the

Exhibit 1. Program timetable.

Project	January	February	March	April	May	June
1. Financial Communications	Sales projection announcement	Quarterly statement		Publish annual report	Annual meeting	
2. Employee Communications		Income tax clinic	Publish newsletter		Fitness clinic	Publish newsletter
3. Community Relations	Prepare for auction	Fund-raising auction	Branch opening reception	Branch opening reception		

executive vice president, or a division vice president? What are they looking for in a budget in terms of explanation?

It is helpful in learning the budgeting system to become acquainted with the accountants in the organization. They can be invaluable in helping you prepare your budget. As key members of the management team, they can point out budget pitfalls to avoid and also instruct you in the organization's accounting procedures. Consulting with the accountants also allows you to explain your position and thinking to them—before any battle lines are drawn.

Here are some basic ways to cultivate controllers and make allies of accountants:

o Use the correct forms for payroll, purchasing, travel expenses.
o Follow routine procedures, but make sure you also can control them—that is, authorize and allocate expenditures.
o Be on time in submitting budgets or other necessary figures.
o Pay attention to detail.

There are many different budgeting systems in use. In some business organizations, such as banks and some consumer packaged goods companies, budgeting procedures are very detailed and inflexible. Other organizations may approach budgeting with less adherence to strict procedures.

PUT THE FIGURES INTO A USABLE FORMAT

After you have a plan and have learned the budgeting system, the next step is to begin putting down some costs on paper.

Though you may have to use specific budget terminology and format for internal purposes, the most useful budget structure is the one that most closely corresponds to your day-to-day operations. Perhaps the easiest way to organize a budget is in terms of administrative costs and functional costs, as in Exhibit 2.

Administrative costs are the costs of operating the department. They should be fairly quick to develop and include salaries (professional and clerical), office supplies, overhead (rent, utilities, etc.), and travel and miscellaneous expenses. Recent past expendi-

Exhibit 2. Internal public relations budget.

Administrative Costs

Salaries		$130,000
Office Supplies		15,000
Overhead		30,000
Travel, Miscellaneous Expenses		25,000
	Subtotal	$200,000

Functional Costs

Financial Communications		$250,000
Employee Communications		75,000
Community Relations		145,000
Product Publicity		50,000
Government Relations		90,000
	Subtotal	$610,000

Contingency		$ 90,000
	TOTAL	$900,000

tures probably are your best guidelines here. Salaries will constitute the largest portion of administrative costs, perhaps as much as 80 percent. Thus, any proposed increase in staff size should be well documented.

Functional costs are those incurred in carrying out the duties and assignments of the public relations function and are directly related to the activities listed in your plan. They may include an annual report, employee publication, community relations programs, and product promotions.

For some projects, such as annual reports, expenditures in past years will be your best guide. Obtain estimates from suppliers: artists, printers, photographers, mailing house, film company, and so on. If outside counsel is to be used, budget for those services.

Since you will most likely be budgeting 6 to 18 months in advance of some time period, allow for inflation in your calculations. Set aside approximately 10 percent of your budget for a contingency fund. It is the nature of public relations to deal with the unexpected, so give yourself flexibility.

Once you have all your figures in place, check with the accountants to see if your numbers are acceptable. They may be able to point out changes that will help approval of the entire budget.

When you present the budget to your superior or budget committee, be prepared to explain any significant budget increases or the shifting of funds from one area to another. This presentation should include a recap of the prior year's budget and cost effectiveness analysis. If you decide to build staff and budgets, your increased expenditures must be based on solid reasoning. As your department and budget grow, you become more visible and perhaps more vulnerable to budget reductions. Staff size is usually, but not always, related to the organization's size and structure and the nature of its business. The issue of internal staff growth versus external counsel assistance will be discussed in the second section of this chapter.

After presenting your initial budget recommendation, one or several revisions may be necessary. Carefully choose the items you will want to defend vigorously. Avoid going to the wrestling mat over details. Occasionally, organization-wide budget cuts on a percentage basis will be mandated by a budget committee or chief executive officer. Your only alternative then is to comply and cope as best you can. When the final figures are in, you may not get everything you want, but if your preparation has been thorough you should get everything you need.

After the budget has been approved, inform your staff, agency, and suppliers about the funds that will be available for their activities so they are aware of spending limits. Plan to monitor the expenditure of funds continuously through the year. This can be valuable in adjusting a budget at midyear and in planning the following year's budget.

MONITOR THE SPENDING

The budget process does not end when the CEO's imprimatur is placed on your budget for the year. Monitoring must be constant to make sure that staff and suppliers are staying within their budget limits, that costs are accounted for, and that problems are all spotted as far in advance as possible.

A simple method to monitor spending is to use a monthly budget flowchart to show the costs incurred each month and the balance of funds remaining for the year. An example of such a chart is given in Exhibit 3. Since administrative costs are incurred in relatively even amounts throughout the year, a budget flowchart is more important for functional costs.

With a budget flowchart, you will be better equipped to detect budget overruns or inaccurate estimates before they become problems.

Checking your budget flowchart against a program timetable (described earlier) will enable you to determine if your expenditures are in line with your scheduled activities. Think of the budget flowchart as a budget early warning system. If you have already spent 75 percent of your financial communications budget by February and you still have the annual report to publish in April, you know that you either are spending too much or budgeted too little for this part of your program.

Many organizations require a midyear budget review and revision. This assignment is made easier by a program timetable and budget flowchart. You may find it necessary to cut back in some areas or ask for additional funding in others.

Near the end of the year, you should be able to determine from the flowchart if your budget estimates were too high, too low, or on target for various activities. This can serve as a guide for planning your next year's budget.

MEASURE AND REPORT THE RESULTS

Measuring and reporting the results of your public relations program are essential in securing the necessary funds for your opera-

Exhibit 3. **Budget flowchart.**

Function	Annual Budget	January Costs	Balance	February Costs	Balance
1. Financial Communications	$250,000	$10,000	$240,000	$20,000	$220,000
2. Employee Communications	75,000	5,000	70,000	2,000	68,000
3. Community Relations	145,000	15,000	130,000	25,000	105,000
4. Product Publicity	50,000	2,000	48,000	3,000	45,000
5. Government Relations	90,000	10,000	80,000	5,000	75,000
Total	$610,000	$42,000	$568,000	$55,000	$513,000

tion. Results must be reported as well as measured or they are of little value to anyone.

Measurement criteria should be established with the understanding and agreement of top management. As public relations director, you should inform management of how you intend to measure the results of your activities and to weigh those results against the monies spent to obtain them. It is important that you develop your own measurement yardsticks. Otherwise, you may be forced to use those of others.

Measurement criteria will vary for each activity. Some activities will be easier to measure than others. Measurement standards may be quantitative, qualitative, or a combination of both. A quantitative measurement could be the amount of publicity coverage obtained for the introduction of a new product. A qualitative measurement could be the local newspaper's editorial reaction to the company's position on an environmental issue.

Although measurement criteria will differ widely among activities, they should be correlated to the expenditures and overall objectives of the public relations program. Measuring results will help answer some of the questions about the current budget and also the next year's. For example, were the security analysts meetings worth the $30,000 it cost to hold them? Why or why not? Was television publicity the most cost efficient way of promoting our new product? How many people did we reach with our message, and what was the cost?

No attempt will be made in this chapter to list all the possible measurement criteria one could use to gauge the results of public relations activities. However, equating publicity results to advertising dollar value for television, radio, or print coverage should be approached cautiously. Avoid this measurement unless you are specifically requested to use it by management. Public relations and advertising are separate functions. They deliver messages in entirely different formats. Any publicity versus advertising dollar comparison is weak at best and misleading at worst.

Measuring results will aid budget decisions for both current and future programs. For example, if the first of three scheduled media promotional tours featuring a corporate spokesperson did not generate enough coverage to justify its cost, the remaining tours might be canceled and funds applied to another activity.

The budgeting process has now come full circle. Analysis of the current year's budget and results will provide the financial foundation for next year's program. Planning and budgeting are ongoing processes, supplying checks and balances that are required to keep a public relations program on target.

The second part of this chapter deals with budgeting for outside public relations counsel and its integration into your budget management.

BUDGETING FOR EXTERNAL COUNSEL

External counsel can enhance and strengthen a public relations program if the agency's role is clearly defined and well managed. The agency can supply people with special expertise that the public relations director does not now have and will not be able to add to the internal staff.

Budget Justification for Counsel

The nature of the internal staff and the internal policy concerning outside counsel can be a major factor in the decision to hire an agency or consultant. Although organizations have many different reasons for hiring outside counsel and justifying the cost, the following corporate examples typify three common approaches to agencies.

Foremost-McKesson, Inc., headquartered in San Francisco, is a large multidivisional company. It distributes chemicals, drugs, and such well-known liquor brands as Galliano and Ballantine's Scotch and manufactures many consumer and institutional food products, including dairy foods, macaroni, powdered garlic and chili, instant hot cocoa, and bottled drinking water. Sales from these operations amount to $3.5 billion. Five companies and many divisions are under its corporate umbrella across the United States.

The corporation's relatively small public relations staff of only five professionals is responsible for financial communications and investor relations, including quarterly and annual reports and security analysts meetings; corporate and individual company identity and publicity programs; a quarterly employee magazine; public affairs, including a quarterly nutrition publication; and community relations. To service the corporation, Foremost-McKesson's public relations department, which has a $1.5 million budget, buys many outside services from agencies, freelance writers, and other suppliers. The company retains one agency on a full-time fee basis and assigns projects to another agency and individual suppliers. Most of Foremost-McKesson's functional budget is spent externally.

"We want to keep a lean staff," James S. Cohune, director of public relations, explained in an interview, "and to do that means spending money on the outside. We feel this gives us more flexibility than building up a large internal staff and budget. A lean staff also makes it easier to justify outside assistance, especially in crisis situations."

Bank of America, the world's largest bank, is at the opposite end of the pole in terms of use of outside public relations counsel. The bank has a budget of several million dollars and more than 100 people worldwide in its corporate communications division, which performs a wide range of activities.

John J. Bell, senior vice president of corporate communications, reports that the bank is an exception among banks in its policy toward agencies.

> Because of our large internal staff, we involve agencies only occasionally on projects, depending on the availability of our own time, people, and expertise. We consciously have developed extensive internal capabilities because we feel it suits our corporate structure and meets our communications objectives.

Clorox Company, a diversified manufacturer of household and institutional products with sales of more than $1 billion, has a staff of seven public relations professionals working in the areas of corporate communications and community affairs and a public relations budget of approximately $500,000. Its public relations staff handles corporate communications; community affairs; employee communications, including publications and employee economic education; financial communications and investor relations (though these costs are paid for by another department); speechwriting; and special events.

Clorox has no set policy regarding agencies. According to Frederick A. Reicker, manager of corporate communications, the company usually calls upon an agency on a project basis when its own staff is short of people, time, expertise, or all three.

At large corporations with small public relations departments, such as those at Foremost-McKesson and Clorox, company presidents, marketing directors, or brand managers may hire agencies on their own. This is usually done with the advice of the public relations director. In such cases, the agency expenditures are paid from the budget of a department other than the corporate public relations department. Similarly, other public relations costs may also be paid by different departments. The annual report cost, for example, might be paid from the budget of the financial vice president. Obviously, the public relations department's budget may not reflect the total amount of money a corporation is spending on public relations.

When you decide to retain an agency, and assign it certain tasks, you must determine how the agency will be paid and how you will budget for its services.

How Agencies Budget

In preparing an estimated budget for a client, public relations agencies determine the cost of the public relations program or list of services approved by the client. Agencies have two major costs: staff time, and production and out-of-pocket expenses. The first is usually the higher by far.

Staff time is the time the public relations agency's professionals devote to develop and implement a program for a client. The cost of staff time in a budget will depend upon (1) the nature of the client's public relations program; (2) the number and rank of staff people servicing the account; and (3) hourly billing rates of account personnel (generally ranging today from $30 to $100 per hour). Public relations agencies charge for services in much the same manner as law and accounting firms do. Staff time is a public relations firm's main source of income.

In addition to staff time, there usually are production costs for such services as printing, artwork, and photography. Many agencies charge a 17.65 percent commission on production costs. This markup is comparable to the 15 percent commission on advertising charged by agencies. The former is a commission added to the net cost rather than deducted from the gross cost.

For example, if a printer charges $850 for a brochure, a public relations agency will add on the 17.65 percent commission. The cost to the client will be $1,000. When an advertising agency buys newspaper space costing $1,000, the client is charged $1,000, but the agency pays only $850 after its 15 percent commission is deducted. Advertising agencies normally bill clients in advance and deduct their commissions before paying media costs. Public relations firms usually bill clients after paying suppliers. In handling production, a public relations agency incurs costs, pays out money, and loses investment interest before being reimbursed. The 17.65 percent commission helps make the waiting easier. Most agencies do not add commission to such minor out-of-pocket costs as travel, postage, and photocopying.

Why pay both staff time and commission? Isn't this a double charge? Not really. Staff time and commission charges are two entirely different cost factors at a public relations agency. The 15 percent commission pays for advertising agency staff time on a $10 million account. The 17.65 percent commission does not pay for staff time on a $10,000 brochure project. Advertising agencies derive most of their income from media commissions. Public relations agencies obtain their income from billing for staff time.

Staff time usually will account for 40 to 80 percent of a public relations program handled by an agency. The explanation for this is that when you hire an agency you are buying peoples' time and talents. Occasionally, large production items will be part of the agency budget.

How Agencies Bill

Basically, public relations firms use two types of budget arrangements: a project budget or an annual budget. For a project budget, the agency may bill a lump sum if the assignment is of short duration. For a lengthy project, monthly invoices will be submitted to the client.

Annual budgets can be handled in two ways: a fee arrangement with fixed monthly payments or monthly billing for actual staff time as it is incurred. To illustrate, if you allocate $120,000 on a fee basis for an agency to spend over a year's time, you can arrange to be billed in 12 installments of $10,000 or 12 invoices of different amounts. Either arrangement would result in a total billing of $120,000 at the end of the year. The fixed fee allows you to budget agency costs and cash flow throughout the year. The monthly progress method more accurately reflects workload and expenditure periods.

Different fee arrangements are available. Some agencies may charge a monthly fee to cover all costs. Others will use a fee plus expenses and additional staff time. Some large agencies have a minimum budget level for clients, especially those on fee accounts. However, most are flexible in working out budgets and billing arrangements.

In any event, you and the agency should have a clear understanding and agreement on the type of billing arrangement before any work is started and costs are incurred by the agency. If you have a question about billing or a cost estimate, you are entitled to a complete answer. Be wary of the agency with vague answers.

Managing an Agency Budget

Here are some guidelines to follow in managing an agency's budget for maximum efficiency and effectiveness.

1. Be sure the agency's budget is completely included in your internal budget and that there is no duplication of expenditures.

2. The agency should be willing and able to document and explain all charges. However, do not have the agency spend an inordinate amount of time documenting and reporting expenses. The net result can be a waste of money.

3. On monthly progress accounts, it may be advisable to have the agency prepare a budget status report, similar to your internal budget flowchart. This will help keep track of spending. Additionally, you should consider having the agency submit a written monthly activities report to substantiate invoices and charges for staff time.

4. Be flexible. Allow for a contingency on budget estimates. Many public relations expenses are difficult to predict.

5. Be open to budget revisions. Budgeting is an evolving effort and must be adjusted to the needs of the organization and new situations.

6. Pay agencies and suppliers promptly. Agency enthusiasm can wane on an account that is constantly delinquent in payments. Prompt payment is good management and good business.

7. Do not ask the agency to absorb or bury costs that are not budgeted or to supply more services than your budget allows. On the other hand, be sure you get the services your budget deserves.

8. Measure the agency's results and relate the results to expenditures.

9. When budget cuts are contemplated, warn the agency as far in advance as possible. The agency should be equally prompt in notifying you about possible budget overages or other problems.

10. Work closely with the agency in developing new programs and relating them to the budget. Much time and effort can be wasted planning activities you cannot afford.

An agency working with a well-managed program and budget can make a substantial contribution in achieving your public relations objectives.

4: News Media Relations

NEWS MEDIA RELATIONS is something like baseball. On the field of play, there's an adversary relationship that must be understood. The "hardball" nature of both endeavors is evident from time to time. and both are governed by rules—written and unwritten—and tradition. There are many positions to be covered and varying degrees of skill among players. Calls of "foul" and "fair" are subjective, and knowing how to win and lose gracefully means a lot to the reputation of the "team." The performances of public relations managers and those in the dugouts affect whether or not they are eventually labeled "major league." And in both cases, consistency and evenhandedness win respect and pennants.

What Is News?

A PR manager must learn what, in general, separates news from non-news and strive mightily to keep material in the latter category out of the information stream. The dissemination of non-news is one of the most insidious deterrents to good media relations. Inevitably, there are times when it cannot be avoided. But building a reputation as the source of adequate, factual, and timely information for the news media depends on one's own ability to distinguish non-news from news and keep the former to oneself. If there is a single principle governing the whole process of coexisting with the news media, it is: "Know what makes news and you'll survive."

There are, of course, other prerequisites to successful news media relations. A prominent newspaper editor spoke about them during a recent appearance at a midwestern university.

"There is no substitute for direct and frequent contact with news people as a means of improving your press relations . . . access is the first key. Honesty is the vital ingredient. . . . Stonewalling is the first sin, but deception is even more dangerous," he said.

In addressing the topic of alleged antibusiness bias in news media, he asked, "Why is it that government officials, politicians, labor union chiefs, environmental activists, social workers, and others have a more symbiotic relationship with the press than business? Is it because their problems are less complex, or that they are more cunning in dealing with newsmen?"

"No, I think not," he continued. "I think the difference is that those people have a better understanding of what the press needs and wants and recognize that it is in their interest to work with journalists, even at the risk of an occasional bruise or bonehead play."

In other words, they know how to play the game. A cynic might say they know how to manipulate the media.

Making Yourself Known

It is assumed that any new personalities on a PR team will make themselves known to the news media people they will be working with. This applies also to anyone who has recently acquired the overall responsibility for a public relations department or operation. A new PR director or manager should make sure that those in the news media know who has certain responsibilities within the PR department. Pocket cards or small brochures that list topical or geographic areas of responsibility can be helpful to journalists. It's important for the news media to know that Joe Jones is the spokesperson for events within Plant A and Sue Smith for Plant B. After-hours and emergency numbers should be part of the listings.

Because of the turnover and rotation of assignments in the news field, as well as in corporate ranks, it is well to assist journalists in knowing whom to contact for company news.

The News Release

The intricacies of creating a news release are not part of this chapter. Suffice it to say that the rules of accuracy and good journalism apply. Textbooks on the subject abound. Sympathetic working journalists are good resources on the finer practical points of the news release. Just don't besiege them with questions or expect unlimited consulting service.

Once the labors of executing the document have ended and the release is sent out, abandon "pride of authorship." The important thing is that the basic information is disseminated. Hemingway's news copy was edited and rewritten. Yours will be too. You should be prepared to complain, however, if your release is misinterpreted, but it is wise to direct your complaint directly to the writer rather than his boss. Consistent errors should be called to the attention of the editors.

Other Handout Materials

Printed news releases are only part of the public relations materials that are sent to the news media. Films, videotapes, audiotapes, slides, and brochures are also used. If you need to use an unfamiliar PR vehicle, get professional help. Credibility—the basis of good news media relations—is damaged by inferior or amateurish efforts. You should be aware that too lavish or wasteful a production or distribution can draw criticism. If you aren't sure, for example, whether a publication can use color transparencies or if a television news director uses supplied film, ask. Continued submission of unwanted or wrong types of information materials indicates carelessness and lack of understanding and an unwillingness to learn the requirements and formats of various media.

Delivery Systems

After information is prepared for release, the obvious next step is to deliver it to the news media. Getting your materials into the hands of those who will use them should be treated like the delivery of other forms of merchandise. Hand delivery by a professional staff member, rather than a messenger service, can underscore the importance of the content. Here are some commonsense guidelines:

1. Ask for the person you want by name. This shows you did your homework.
2. Don't oversell your material. Put all the effort you can into preparation.
3. Make sure you or other follow-up contacts are clearly identified on the material.
4. Be certain that the phone numbers are correct and that someone knowledgeable will be there to answer calls.
5. Be fair about the timing of releases you know will be of interest. If you are delivering information to competing news media, try to arrange simultaneous delivery.

Screen mailing lists carefully. This is never a particularly interesting task, but it should get the same attention as payroll lists. Lists should be updated at least annually. Use returned mail to eliminate old or incorrect addresses, and send self-addressed, stamped postcards periodically to find out if the recipients want to remain on your lists.

Journalists have stories galore about mail they get addressed to defunct publications, deceased colleagues, and garbled names and titles—none of them particularly helpful to the credibility of the information in the releases or of your company.

Media Directories

Various publications describe the formats, personnel, locations, coverage areas, and other characteristics of almost all news media. Some of those used most commonly are:

Working Press of the Nation—a five-volume paperback series covering newspapers, magazines, TV and radio, feature writers, photographers, syndicates, and internal publications.

Ayer Directory of Publications—single-volume hardbound listing of daily and weekly newspapers and consumer, business, technical, professional, trade, and farm magazines; particularly useful in finding all publications in a city.

Bacon's Publicity Checker—separate spiral-bound volumes for magazines and newspapers; helpful in identifying types of editorial materials accepted, such as by-lined articles, product information, photos.

Editor and Publisher International Yearbook—six-part single paperback volume listing U.S., Canadian, and foreign newspapers, syndicated services, and publishing industry organizations and services.

Broadcasting Yearbook—annual publication of *Broadcasting* magazine; lists U.S. areas of TV coverage, ownership, call letters of radio and TV stations, and formats, for example, religious, all-news, rock, top-40.

Hudson's Washington News Media Contacts Directory—lists bureaus, correspondents, personnel, and departments of Washington print and broadcast media; a D.C. essential.

Television Contacts and *Radio Contacts*—separate paperback directories of news and public affairs programming and hosts, staffs, directors, and the like.

Standard Rate & Data Service—monthly paperback volumes, primarily advertising oriented for space/time cost estimation, covering newspapers, radio, TV, consumer and farm magazines, and business and trade publications; useful because of monthly updating of names and addresses.

Regional guides are also available through such organizations as clipping bureaus, state newspaper or broadcasters associations, and commercial sources. List brokers, too many to enumerate here, can usually be found in the Yellow Pages of telephone books under "mailing lists." They frequently can supply news media listings for broad-scale distributions.

Newswires

Newswires, also known as wire services, are intermedia networks that develop and transmit information used in publications or the electronic media. They do not publish or broadcast information.

Their services are purchased by the "end-user" medium. Newswire coverage is vitally important. A single news story transmitted on a wire service is reviewed by editors at every subscribing news outlet.

News services use circuits to segregate information of national, statewide, regional, or city interest. Written text sent by teleprinters is the most common format, although photographic facsimile and audio services for radio broadcasters are available. Nearly all newspapers and broadcasters subscribe to a wire service.

The Associated Press and United Press International are the only major general newswires in the United States. Dow Jones and Reuters are national newswires specializing in financial and business information.

News service bureaus can be found in every state capital and most major cities. Depending on bureau size, they may have specialized reporters covering such beats as government, sports, business and finance, science, courts, environment, and transportation.

A growing number of services are offered by private newswires, which place data terminals in newspaper and broadcast newsrooms. Publicists pay a fee for use of their circuits. Such services transmit information verbatim and on a known schedule. Conventional newswires, in contrast, rewrite almost all submitted copy and may hold information for comment from other sources or as the basis for a later story.

Newswires are competitive and pride themselves on moving a story even a few minutes in advance of each other. Precedence indicators are assigned, from "flash" (reserved for only the most important news stories and not often used) to "bulletin" and "urgent." This makes it important for public relations practitioners to deliver materials to competing bureaus simultaneously, or as nearly as possible. Financial information for Reuters and Dow Jones is usually telephoned.

Wire services operate constantly, unlike newspapers or broadcast news, which have specified times for editions or programs. Each bureau has daily routines and cycles that should be known by PR managers who deal with them.

Newswires have their own procedures, terminology, and copy styles. Journalism textbooks and histories of the major wire services can provide additional background on how they developed and operate. Stylebooks can be purchased directly from the services and at most college bookstores. Most bureau managers are happy to give brief explanations of their operations if it helps them maintain contact with news sources. But remember, they're truly "always on deadline" and don't have much time for "guided tours."

Wire service coverage results in fast, wide distribution of information directly to the news media in a form ready for use. It merits special attention from PR managers.

News Conferences

Nearly every public relations manager must sooner or later hold a news conference. Several criteria apply.

1. A news conference should be reserved for truly major announcements. More than two or three per year, except during a crisis, is probably excessive for a business or corporate sponsor.

2. The most senior management available should conduct the main part of the news conference, but only after thorough familiarization with the subject matter and rehearsal(s).

3. As part of the planning, attention must be paid to every physical detail, such as access to the conference site (particularly if within a large corporate operation), physical and climatic conditions (heating, cooling, light, shelter from elements if outdoors, noise levels, etc.), and fully tested microphones and sound systems, projectors, and other audiovisual aids, complete with trained operators and spare bulbs.

4. Brief but complete announcements for invitations to news media should be sent 10 days to two weeks in advance. It is wise to make telephone calls as reminders one or two days before the event. Self-addressed reply postcards are an optional RSVP.

5. Adequate numbers of complete information packages, including full speech texts, captioned photos, and charts, should be on hand for distribution at the beginning of the conference and follow-up distribution later to no-shows. (Press kits will be discussed more fully in the next section.)

When skillfully executed, a news conference can create news coverage of very large proportions. Major disappointments can occur, however, caused—not infrequently—by unforseen news breaking elsewhere.

Some refreshments should be provided, such as coffee and doughnuts, perhaps a buffet lunch, and even more at major events. What you provide in the way of snacks can affect the overall impression of the event, for better or worse, but it should never be considered so much of an inducement that reporters will come just to eat. If you decide to serve liquor, don't open the bar until after the conference and bear in mind that tipsy journalists may enjoy themselves but don't always file the best stories.

Press Kits

A press kit is an assembly of materials that each news media representative can take away from a news conference. Typically, it is a paper folder or jacket containing several items, usually a news release, speech text, captioned photos or charts, and perhaps a description of the conference sponsor. A standard temptation is to stuff more information into it than is needed, such as the company's annual report, large photos of many corporate officers who did not participate in the conference, internal newsletters, sales literature, even bumper stickers, keychains, or whatever else is around. Some reporters will take everything. Most prefer to stick to the basics and will ask for any additional materials they need.

Press kits are valuable for follow-up distribution to important news conference no-shows and can be important supplements to journalists who are not accompanied by photographers or who want to review a speech or other data. They are not required for every news release. Useful, adequate, and well-thought-out press kits are a mark of professionalism and a sign that the needs of the news media are understood.

Follow-up

A reporter's decision to use or not to use information issued at a news conference or in a news release may depend on further verification or clarification. It is imperative that informed spokespersons be available at the telephones listed in the news materials. If your material is such that another party may be called to verify data, such as a government agency you have quoted or whose statistics are used, it is absolutely essential for you to let that party know what you are doing. All your efforts at securing news attention can be undone by a third-party expert who tells a journalist, "I don't know where they got that information."

There may be instances when you need to know whether news coverage will appear. Such queries should be low-pressure, not sales jobs. A simple "Were you able to use the information?" should draw an adequate response. If the answer is "no," you may ask why. But beyond that, your reaction may be interpreted as an infringement on the professional judgment of a reporter or editor. You may get personal satisfaction from venting your frustration, but it's more likely to "poison the well" you must go back to.

Lastly, if you get calls from reporters at any time, you should observe this canon of news media relations: Always call back.

Timing and Deadlines

Learn the deadline requirements of the news media with which you have frequent contact. You can be the source of much frustration if you walk into a newspaper office with a good story five minutes after the deadline of the last edition. Similarly, don't hope to interest a television assignment editor in anything routine for that night's news if its after 2 P.M.

Such information can be helpful on those occasions when you are required to issue "bad" news. Newspapers are typically smaller and read less widely on Saturday than on other days of the week, so release bad news on Friday afternoon. Monday morning is traditionally the time when there is the least news breaking and a release has the best chance of being picked up. Release "good" news then.

A news conference scheduled for 10 A.M. Monday through Thursday stands a better chance of being well attended than a similar event held later in the day or on a Friday.

Trade Conferences and Pressrooms

Most major trade conferences, conventions, and exhibitions have a pressroom where information packages are made available to the media. Pressroom use is usually limited to exhibitors or other participants and is not a room for sales literature. It is desirable to check these facilities frequently to restock materials if needed and to offer assistance to anyone who may be reviewing your information at the time.

Some basic materials should be on hand in pressrooms at all times, such as the company history, new-product information, or lists of company news contacts. Items that are time sensitive, such as speech texts, can be added after or during their delivery. Since trade editors and reporters are the most frequent visitors to pressrooms, their particular interests should be kept in mind. Nonetheless, they seek new information, so don't place catalogs or routine periodicals in pressrooms.

In addition to serving the trade press, it's good business to contact the business desk of major-event city newspapers, which are usually interested in what's going on in their town even if it is not their standard news fare.

On the Record or Off the Record

You can avoid unhappy misunderstanding by assuming everything you say in the presence of a journalist may be reported. If you want to be sure facts you know are kept confidential, don't talk about them at all. If you have assurances in advance that a discussion or personal opinion will be kept off the record, you can trust that promise as much as you trust the person who gave it. Above all, don't relate sensitive details first and then ask for your remarks to be off the record. It doesn't make much sense for a PR pro to ask for this kind of treatment when all other efforts are designed to gain exposure.

Can You Kill a Story?

Once the proverbial cat is out of the bag, it usually can't be recaptured unless it returns of its own volition.

If you learn that bad news is forthcoming and the facts are correct, roll with the punch and prepare a response. If a report you learn of in advance is false, you can do a real service to a reporter by advising him or her of this and preventing a mistake. Asking for a later correction is not as effective.

Strident protests, however, can reinforce a rumor to the point where it becomes news or can turn fresh attention to issues that might otherwise expire. Threats of libel suits are often heard, usually ignored, and viewed as immature by seasoned journalists. If there is a case, take legal action. Don't just rattle your saber.

Likewise, punitive withdrawal of advertising from a medium in which you feel you have been wronged editorially only offers another opportunity for airing your dirty linen. It also eliminates the chance to reach the same audience with messages you can control. Editors, who operate autonomously, typically resent being reminded that you are an advertiser.

Asking for a retraction, unless you are fully aware of the firmness of your grounds, is also tricky. In some cases, as a former White House deputy press secretary once said, "It's like asking the truck that just ran over you to back up so you can get the license number."

Fielding Investigative Questions

"What would you do if Mike Wallace called you in the morning and Jack Anderson called you after lunch?" That was the subtitle of a seminar sponsored by the Northeast District of the Public Relations Society of America that discussed the impact on business of the trend toward more "detective" work by journalists. The seminar, titled "The Investigative Climate—How It Relates to Your Company," was held in New York City in September 1978. A well-known investigative reporter advised PR pros not to be intimidated by sudden calls, which frequently may be "fishing expeditions." The following rules were suggested.

1. Determine what a reporter can prove before answering questions. Don't ramble, which can provide more information. You can request that questions be put in writing.

2. Asking for more time to answer is legitimate. Many questions must be researched. You can advise a reporter that your work will also benefit him if he is fair and avoids recklessness.

3. Don't go off the record until you are dealing with a reporter you know and whose word is respected. Get a definition of what "off the record" means before you talk.

4. Don't ever lose your temper; assume you are being recorded.

5. Give a written statement instead of seeking a television appearance to reply. An announcer reading the statement avoids the bias automatically attached to a company spokesperson.

6. If an interview, in person or over the phone, becomes necessary concerning a sensitive subject, ask to have your secretary or an assistant on the line or present. You can have your own set of notes taken.

7. If there is an error of fact in news coverage, you have every right to object. You may not get a retraction, but you'll make an important point about your concern for accuracy.

Two active news media representatives at the same seminar, however, disagreed with the go-slow attitude in making press comments. A business magazine editor said that the necessary adversary relationship of the press with business must be recognized. He pointed out that there are always sources of information that will talk about a company, former PR people among them, and that a ready response is best. Passing up a chance to talk forgoes the opportunity to get out all the pro points about a situation and leaves the field wide open to the con viewpoint, which may be the only one that ends up in print or on the air. A television consumer reporter echoed these sentiments. A delayed or absent response is a hindrance to a reporter who is trying to give a balanced presentation. An attorney specializing in libel cases offered a few additional points about playing hardball with the news media.

○ Investigative reporters have no special legal rights that an ordinary citizen does not have; they have a broad defense because of legal interpretations of their neutral reporting, but that's all.
○ You can rightfully respond to any charge, but don't be tempted into countering one falsehood with another.
○ Unless there are special problems, don't let company lawyers write the press release. PR people can't expect to have it all their way either, however.
○ If you are the victim of attack by a politician, respond vigorously and fairly and make the situation known in his or her home district, where it counts most.

Spokesperson Training

Familiarizing corporate management with the techniques and skills required for effective news interviews is a part of news media relations. This training makes it easier for a seasoned PR manager to make management up the line accessible to news media.

Top executives who become known for well-spoken remarks and polished delivery are more likely to be sought for comment, particularly by broadcast journalists. This does not mean automatic access to media platforms, but it is a decided advantage where a choice exists between a smooth speaker and an amateur.

Realistic training sessions are of great value in preparing spokespersons for actual interviews. Various training programs are available through major public relations agencies and specialized speaker training services or in house at large corporations. Many of the courses are conducted in television studios, with videotape running and interviews conducted by former or freelance news talent. Planned questioning leads the interviewee over verbal "landmines" relating to a relevant subject or corporate issue. Such practice sessions can promote fluency in getting a point across and desensitize the speaker to hostile questioning that might otherwise cause anger or confusion.

Ethics—Gifts and Gratuities

Ever since Adam bit that apple, people have wondered if there is more to a gift than meets the eye. News people are particularly sensitive to this. No reputable journalist can be bought for the price of a lunch, dinner, or an occasional small remembrance. Policy set by news media management, however, interprets what is suitable for staff members to accept. In some instances, nothing is allowed.

In the case of travel and lodging for working press invited to a distant location, make it apparent at the outset what the sponsor will pay for. It is usual to offer all-expense-paid arrangements. However, a growing number of media representatives have travel budgets of their own to eliminate criticism about "junketeering." If they are policy-bound to operate within such financial limits, this makes them highly selective of what they will cover in person.

Cultivating a courteous working relationship with members of the news media usually allows them to be your guests on occasion for meals, press parties, receptions, open houses, tours, or other social or semisocial functions. The purpose of any of these is simply to open channels of communication. More than that should not be expected.

Trade Press—A Different Breed

Trade publications, which cover specific industries, products, or services, require the same basic care and feeding as general circulation news media. Because of their well-defined audiences, they may be the most important medium to a business. A company in the foundry business, for example, may consider *Foundry* magazine akin to holy writ.

The relatively narrow field of interest of most trade publications creates a constant need for detailed information about activities, products, and individuals within that field. Trade publications often use specific product application and case history features that would not be of interest to general business writers. There is a competition for coverage in most trade publications, and all editorial submissions or contacts must be governed by the usual news guidelines and presented in the most usable format.

While the headquarters for trade publications are concentrated in major cities, bureaus and correspondents are spread across the business landscape of America. A thorough media relations program should involve contact with such regional representatives and knowledge of their news interests and responsibilities.

Round-up and Wrap-up Stories

Business and trade publications occasionally review an entire industry or field of activity of which your company may be only a part. Such generic stories are sometimes tied in with special advertising sections. Advertising space sales representatives can provide early warning of such special sections or issues. Alert PR managers will then quickly respond with relevant editorial material. While individual companies or products might receive little more than a mention in this type of article, high-quality photography—supplied by the PR manager—is frequently a key to additional exposure and, in some instances, the cover photo.

Exclusives

The decision to give information to a single publication on an exclusive basis is usually a matter of priorities. The largest, most prestigious publication among a field of several others might ask for and receive such treatment. Exclusives may also be offered as an inducement to editorial coverage.

If dealing on an exclusive basis, take pains to respect the agreement. This usually means waiting until coverage appears before disseminating any form of the same information elsewhere. Even the hint of breaking the agreement may quash a story and damage the potential for such treatment in the future.

Some Final Hints

A veteran New Jersey journalist has offered these suggestions for developing good news media relations. They may have application to other areas as well.

- Learn geography; for example, where are *The Jersey Journal, Bergen Record,* and Newark *Star-Ledger* in relation to each other? Make a postcard check of editors to find out where their interests are.
- Don't overkill on mailings; wasted materials are resented. One release to a specific person is sufficient. Be sure photos are sharp black-and-white prints (for most newspapers).
- Never submit fill-in-the-blank releases.
- Avoid being coy about invitations to events; give specific details before expecting a decision on whether a staffer will be assigned.
- Know what separates editorial material from advertising.

Another journalist adds these tips:

- "Read our paper. I would like a dollar for every press agent who has said to me, 'I don't read your paper.' If you read us, you'll know what we need."
- "Don't lie to us. You can exaggerate a little, but don't send 20 releases to 20 different staff writers without telling us. That is a form of lying."
- "Don't call me or one of your clients a gal. This is a purely personal prejudice, but when I hear it my mind shuts off. 'Honey' and 'dear' are also red-flag words with me."
- "Please don't ask me for tear sheets, because we are in the business of selling newspapers not giving them away."

Finally, news people come in all sizes, shapes, and colors. Some are much smarter and some are much dumber than non-news people. The wisest attitude to have is that they are your peers and colleagues. They are in the information business, and so are you. If you can't accept these conditions as a PR manager, look for a new line of work.

5: Industrial Product Publicity

THE PURPOSE of industrial product publicity is to support sales.

The cost of a sales call in today's economy is high. Cold canvassing is expensive—usually an act of last resort for an industrial salesman. The salesman is far more successful if he calls on people who have inquired about his company's products and who might be ready to buy.

A well-planned and -executed product publicity program will generate valuable sales leads. It will create an awareness in the marketplace of your company's name, products, capabilities, channels of distribution, and personnel. Product publicity can develop and maintain a preferential attitude among customers and prospects for your company's products. And it can supply the basis for effective communications between the home office, field sales, distributors and dealers, and customers.

Product publicity is good for a salesman's morale. He appreciates getting leads, knowing that the home office is working to make his job easier. He gets a psychological boost when he walks into a customer's office and hears, "Oh yes, I saw an article about your product in *Design News* last week." He has a discussion point.

The generation of sales leads is also a major function of advertising. However, there are several major differences between product advertising and product publicity.

With advertising, you buy the space in a magazine, newspaper, or other media. Your message is printed, word for word, as written. You make exactly the points you want to make about your product. You can run the advertisement week after week, month after month for as long as you want. The publication is happy to receive the income.

Publicity, on the other hand, is written in news style by your public relations staff and sent to the editor as a news story for possible use in the editorial pages of his publication. There is no guarantee that the editor will use it. If he does, he may change it—sometimes drastically. This is the editor's prerogative, so long as he does not materially alter the facts. That rarely happens. Bear in mind that your public relations person has sent him a news release which is free information. If the editor prints it, your company has obtained an important audience for its product story. But you have little control over if, when, or how much of the submitted material will be used.

Another difference between advertising and publicity is that once an editor uses a story, he is not likely to ever use it again. It's normally a one-shot deal.

News releases do not get a cold reception, however. For the most part, they are read and evaluated by the trade press. Editors rely heavily on publicity material to fill out their issues. Few, if any, industrial publications today have editorial staffs large enough to cover everything that's happening in their industry. Editors seek and welcome assistance from competent public relations people.

A major benefit of product publicity, as compared with advertising, is believability. A product story that appears in the editorial pages has been evaluated by an editor. There is an implied sanction that the product will perform as described. It is, in effect, a third-party endorsement.

This element of believability is not always present in advertising. Readers often are wary of advertising claims. Ads do not have the third-party objectivity of editorial material. A product publicity story will often generate many more sales leads than an ad for the same product.

Another important advantage of product publicity is the range of distribution. Few companies have advertising budgets large enough to permit scheduling a product ad in every medium where there is likely to be reader interest. In comparison, the cost of reproducing multiple copies of a news release and mailing them to 100 or 200 publications is inconsequential.

Commodity Versus Proprietary Products

The kind of products your company manufactures directly affects the potential for publicity of those products. If your company is in a growth industry, such as electronics, and has a successful product research and development effort, product publicity opportunities will abound. Product publicity is more difficult for a company that manufactures standard products, such as heavy-duty truck axles and drive shafts, whose designs have changed little over the years.

Industrial products generally can be classified into two categories: proprietary and commodity types. A proprietary product is usually patented or otherwise protected. Proprietary products, because of their uniqueness, are relatively easy to publicize.

Commodity products, such as coal, cement, lumber, and bulk chemicals, present a greater publicity challenge because of their sameness. They are usually processed to industry or government standards. Regardless of who produces it, there is little discernible difference in, say, No. 1 white pine lumber, or hydrochloric acid, or Type 302 stainless steel. Publicity opportunities for commodity products generally are limited to superior service offered by the manufacturer, price advantages, and "coattail" case histories.

Superior service would include such things as fast, reliable delivery; dependable supply during periods of shortages; and finishing operations offered as extras, for example, materials precut and sized to customer specifications or weighed and prepackaged according to customer requirements.

A coattail case history involves developing a publicity article about how a customer is using your commodity product in an important or unusual project. The customer's project is the news peg. Your product goes along for the ride and gets mentioned, perhaps, when the article is published. Many large manufacturers of commodity products do this as a matter of customer relations. The theory is that what's good for their customers is good for them. Coattail case histories increased dramatically during the space program of the 1960s and early 1970s. Similarly, other opportunities were offered by major construction projects such as the Alaska pipeline, the Sears Building in Chicago, and the World Trade Center in New York City. Another example is the concrete-canoe racing competitions that are currently the fad among many engineering colleges. The amount of concrete used in the construction of the canoes is insignificant, but the novelty of the idea is newsworthy and gives cement manufacturers an opportunity to publicize a mundane, albeit important, commodity. There will be more on case histories later in the chapter.

How a Product Publicity Staff Operates

Product publicity is a communications function. In most organizations, this department reports to the company's communications director or public relations director, if such titles exist, with dotted-line responsibility to marketing or sales.

A corporate product publicity staff, whether it consists of one person or 50, will usually develop a publicity program for the year. This program, to be most effective, should be tied to the objectives of the company's marketing plan. The product publicity program serves only as a guide for work to be accomplished during the year. It is not engraved in bronze. The program should be flexible enough to substitute projects and to pursue new publicity opportunities as they develop.

In its day-to-day activities, the staff works closely with marketing, sales, engineering, product development, and legal personnel. The marketing department gives the staff strategic direction: what products or markets should be pursued, need extra support, or should be deemphasized. The sales department supplies tactical information: price changes, new distributors and dealers, promotional programs, a list of customers who are experiencing unusual benefits from use of your products, trade show participation, and other product-related field activities.

The engineering department's role in product publicity is to supply technical information and to verify the accuracy of written material before it is released to the press. The research and development laboratory often performs the same function when new products are ready for introduction.

Review of all publicity material by the legal department is standard operating procedure for many companies, to prevent accidental disclosure of proprietary information and to avoid possible legal problems that could develop from improper wording or misuse of trademarks and so on. Many product publicity people regard lawyers as a barrier to the free flow of information because of their conservative attitude. But, on balance, legal approval of news material is in the company's best interests.

Publicity Tools

A productive publicity staff has available many communications tools for getting information to the marketplace. The most common is the news release, distributed simultaneously to all mass communications media with an interest in a company's industry. In the case of industrial products, the interested media are usually the trade publications.

Nearly all trade publications are eager to receive releases on new products, new literature, new dealers and distributors, major installations, orders or contracts, and price changes. Such news releases are regarded as routine by the product publicity people. They are usually brief and easily produced and distributed.

Another product publicity tool is the technical article that deals with some area of a company's expertise. Usually, a product publicity person will contact an editor to sound out his interest in a particular subject. In some cases, an editor will call the public relations department to request an article. The editor may want to interview technical people and write the story himself. But more often, he will request that the product publicity staff develop the article and submit it under the by-line of the engineer who supplied the information.

The product case history is another product publicity tool, one that has been used quite successfully over the years. The coattail case history was mentioned earlier, but the most effective case histories for your company are those that stand on their own merits and explain how a customer using your product realized direct benefits. These user benefits may be in the form of improved design or product performance or savings in costs, production time, labor, or maintenance. Trade magazine editors like these kinds of stories because they tell what is going on in the industry now and inform readers with similar problems how such problems can be solved.

Customers are usually willing to cooperate when your product publicity staff requests a case history interview. Most managements like to talk about their achievements and see them in print. In some isolated instances, permission will be denied because customers don't want competitors to know what they are doing.

Producing a case history is more expensive than generating an in-house technical article or product news release. It often requires a field trip by a product publicity person and the services of a photographer. Approval by the customer of the final written material and photographs is absolutely essential.

The press conference is an effective tool for introducing an important new product or process. The product must be a significant advancement in technology to qualify for press conference treatment. An editor's time is valuable. If he spends a day or more attending a press conference only to learn that you are introducing a copy of a competitor's existing product, you are liable to get bad press. The credibility of your entire publicity program, product and corporate, will suffer.

Arranging a press conference is a major undertaking, and it's expensive. Ideally, planning should begin several months before the event. A program must be developed, scripts written, audiovisuals prepared, a press kit with news releases and photographs produced, and arrangements made for a meeting room, food, beverages, lodging, and transportation. An editorial guest list must be prepared. Invitations should be sent two to three weeks before the event. Follow-up telephone calls are recommended during the final week to verify attendance by editors and reporters.

A well-conducted press conference can launch a new product like a rocket, obtaining editorial coverage worth many times the cost of the conference. For example, a few years ago a machine tool builder held a press conference to introduce a tape-controlled lathe—the first of its kind in the industry. The company hoped to produce eight of the machines during the first year and sell them at $100,000 each. Within two months after the press conference, all eight had been sold and the sales department was backlogging orders for the following year.

In another instance, a manufacturer of engineering plastics held a press conference to introduce a new process for casting large nylon parts under ambient conditions, without need of high-pressure injection molding machines. It was a true technological breakthrough. The story received feature treatment in the business section of *The New York Times* the next day and was picked up by *The Wall Street Journal,* the wire services, and every major plastics and materials trade publication. The company's sales department was flooded with inquiries, and its new business was off to a flying start.

External house organs—magazines and newsletters that are mailed periodically to customers—are often prepared by the product publicity staff to generate sales leads. A major manufacturer of silicone products has been using this marketing tool successfully for 15 years. The company publishes on alternate months a 12-page magazine that contains case histories and new-product and technical information on a broad range of industrial uses for its silicone materials. The magazine has an international circulation of more than 40,000, mostly to design engineers, manufacturing engineers, production managers, laboratory managers, and industrial purchasing agents. The publication is an expensive project, but each issue generates thousands of inquiries from primary buying influences. Many similar publications are used in industry today.

Internal publications, such as newsletters for field sales personnel, distributors, dealers, and sales representatives, also may require the services of the product publicity staff.

Trade shows are usually the responsibility of the sales promotion
department. However, they, too, offer product publicity opportunities. A trade show is a major industry event; virtually every
important purchaser will attend. Trade magazine editors will be
there to report on developments. This gives product publicity
people an opportunity to have personal contact with many editors
within a short period of time. The sales people who staff the company exhibit are on the lookout for customers, while the product
publicity person is locating editors, steering them to the company
exhibit, and making sure that each editor receives an information
kit on the company's products.

A product publicity person should contact the trade publications
in advance of a trade show to find out who from their editorial staff
is going to attend. Then, he might invite the editor or editors to
meet him at the company's hospitality suite, if there is one, or for
lunch or dinner to discuss feature article ideas. Trade show attendance is important for the product publicity staff effort.

Dealer and distributor activities are potential sources of product
publicity. When the sales department appoints a new distributor,
dealer, or sales representative, a news release announcing the ap-
pointment and the product lines the appointee will carry should be
sent to the trade press. The media mailing list should include regional purchasing, industrial, and business publications and newspapers in the new distributor's or dealer's locale. The regional publications are often receptive to articles about dealer and distributor
activities, particularly if they are involved in supplying products to
an important industry or project in the region. The dealers and
distributors will welcome this kind of support.

Product publicity staff may also aid the activities of other departments. They may produce audiovisual presentations and films
about product performance, operation, and maintenance, to be
shown by field sales people to customers and prospects. The en-

gineering department will often seek assistance from the product publicity staff in preparing speeches and technical papers on product technology for delivery at technical seminars, conferences, and sales meetings.

Merchandising Your Publicity

Earlier it was noted that a publicity story is essentially a one-shot deal. That applies only to the editor and his publication, not to the product publicity staff. Once an article is printed it can be "merchandised."

For example, a trade magazine prints a technical article authored by one of your engineers or a case history submitted by your public relations department. Most trade publications will supply large quantities of reprints at a very reasonable cost; it gives them added exposure, too. Your product publicity staff can then distribute these reprints to the company salesmen for use as "leave behinds" when making sales calls and to dealers for handing out to their customers. Often, the advertising department will use these reprints for direct mail campaigns.

Similarly, clippings of shorter items about your company's products may be collected and reproduced in a flyer or brochure format for use by the sales organization to impress customers. It's also a good idea to distribute these reprinted items internally, to keep other departments in the company aware of the job being done by public relations.

The Media

Most industrial product publicity efforts are directed to trade publications. Newspapers, television, and radio generally are not interested in industrial products unless they are manufactured in a local plant and might possibly mean higher employment in the hometown. In the case of a genuine technological breakthrough, the general news media should be included on the mailing list or invited to the press conference.

More than 3,000 trade and professional magazines and newsletters are published in the United States today. Every industry category is represented. The welding industry, for example, is served by three publications; the medical and health field has more than 200.

Most trade publications are published monthly. There are a few dailies and many weekly, biweekly, semimonthly, and quarterly publications. Some require paid subscriptions. Others are controlled circulation publications; that is, they are sent free to persons employed in the industry served by the publication. Rarely will you see a trade publication for sale on a newsstand, although there are a few exceptions.

Trade magazines are of two general types: vertical and horizontal. A vertical publication serves only one industry or one field of technology. *Microwave Journal, Lubrication Engineering,* and *Foundry* are examples. A horizontal publication prints news concerning all industries. Among these are *Business Week, Fortune,* and *Industry Week.* An even finer distinction can be made: There are horizontal publications within vertical industry categories. *Iron Age* is concerned with all metalworking processes and markets, such as welding, machining, casting, stamping, and finishing, in addition to metallurgy and the steel-making process. *Chemical Week* serves the chemical industry and *Engineering News Record* the construction industry in much the same way.

An important part of the product publicity person's job is to become familiar with the kinds of news items used by each trade publication in his industry. Many publications will publish new-product and new-literature items; others will not. Some want price information; some do not. There are technical publications that publish only by-lined or staff-written articles. The editorial mix varies from one publication to another. An editor is likely to become irritated if he consistently receives new-literature releases from a company although his publication does not publish new-literature information. He knows that the public relations person who mailed the releases has never bothered to read his magazine. To avoid this kind of embarrassment, a well-run product publicity department will compile separate mailing lists for each news-item category. Several trade publication directories are available to simplify this task.

Developing media contacts is an important part of the product publicity person's job. Letters and telephone calls are satisfactory, but nothing can substitute for personal contact. A product publicity person, when he is traveling, should plan to visit with editors on his itinerary. He should make occasional editorial trips expressly to meet and talk shop with editors of major publications in his industry. Editors welcome these visits.

Editors also should be invited individually to visit your company, tour the facilities, and see your production operations firsthand. It's a good idea to have a story idea to offer him, but more likely than not he'll develop a few ideas of his own while touring the plant.

The Scene Overseas

Conducting an international product publicity program can be difficult. One problem is locating the publications; another is the language barrier. Some U.S. trade publications do have circulation in foreign countries, but their coverage is limited.

There are international directories available. However, these tend to become outdated rather quickly. News releases going to non-English-language publications should be translated, rather than submitted in English with the expectation that the foreign editors can read English. The best approach is to hire public relations or advertising agencies in the countries where your company's products are marketed. They can do the translation and distribution of your releases and also obtain clippings of published articles to prove that your publicity is working.

News Dissemination

Product news can be distributed to the news media in a number of ways. Most often it is done through the mail. Compiling a mailing list is extremely important and should not be done haphazardly. Markets for a specific product should be analyzed, and the appropriate publications selected carefully. If important publications are omitted, or wrong publications included, the product publicity job is not being done properly. You may have prepared a great product story and first-rate photographs, but much of the effort will be wasted if the mailing list is incomplete.

Where timing is important, in cases such as major price change announcements, the product publicity staff will use the wire services—Dow Jones, Associated Press, United Press International. Several public relations wire services are available to complement this effort.

The news should be released to all wire services simultaneously, preferably, hand delivered to each office. If the wire services do not have offices in your location, then the news should be phoned to the nearest offices. Dow Jones, AP, and UPI—if they use the information—will usually condense a news release drastically. There is no cost involved.

The public relations wire services will transmit your release in its entirety. A charge is levied based on the length of the release and whether you want regional or national distribution. Many newspapers, publishing houses, and other organizations subscribe to these private wire services, but coverage is by no means universal.

Wire service distribution should also be used when a new product of major significance is introduced.

Feature syndicates, both news and paid-for, offer limited possibilities for industrial product publicity. Newspapers are the principal subscribers to such syndicated material. An industrial product must have broad public appeal to warrant newspaper coverage. Such products are few and far between.

Production Costs

The cost of printing and distributing new-product publicity is relatively small. News releases generally are reproduced by offset printing or photocopying. If a photograph is to accompany the release, then multiple prints should be made. Machine-made prints do not have the same quality as handmade prints but cost considerably less. The type of product and the size of the distribution list are factors in determining which kind of prints to use. Occasionally, line drawings or artists' renderings are required to illustrate a product's design or function. The collating of printed and photographic materials, envelope stuffing, addressing, and mailing may be done in house or performed by a commercial mailing service.

Considerably higher production costs can be expected if the product publicity department uses brochures, films, and other audiovisual aids.

Measuring Results

The results of product publicity are fairly easy to track. The effectiveness of a news release is determined by how many inquiries it generates and how many of these inquiries are converted to sales.

The majority of inquiries will be received in the mail directly from the trade magazines. Many trade magazines contain reader-inquiry cards, enabling the reader merely to circle a number corresponding to a news item in which he is interested. He then mails the postage-paid card to the publisher. The publisher compiles all inquiries pertaining to your product and mails them to your company, usually once a month in the form of a computer printout.

Normally, someone in the public relations, sales, or marketing department is assigned the task of validating these inquiries. This involves crossing out the names of competitors and others who are not likely to be customers. Frequently, inquiries are received from college students. Some companies will send literature to engineering school inquiries on the basis that today's engineering student may be tomorrow's specifier.

If a reader has an immediate need for your product, he is likely to telephone or write directly to your sales department. These leads are then relayed to the field salesmen.

Some publicity organizations assess publicity results by measuring the amount of published space their products have received and then converting the total into what it would have cost for the same amount of advertising space. In the final analysis, however, it is the amount of sales generated that really counts.

Another measuring tool is the market survey. This involves conducting a product awareness survey before a publicity program begins and another after it has been in progress or completed.

Using a PR Agency

There is a right and a wrong way to use the services of an outside public relations agency. Agencies are expensive compared with using internal staff. If you use an agency, avoid assigning routine work and clerical jobs to it wherever possible.

An agency offers an available pool of creative talent and marketing expertise. You can use this expertise in developing the annual product publicity program and for special projects. Use the services of the agency's specialists in audiovisual scriptwriting and production, speech writing, technical writing, and similar areas that require a high degree of creative talent.

An agency can substantially increase your product publicity effort without increasing internal staff, and it can be called upon to help out when the company staff is overloaded.

Our first statement in this chapter was that the purpose of product publicity is to support sales. If your product publicity appears in *The New York Times* or *The Wall Street Journal* and inspires some people to call their stockbrokers with buy orders for your company's stock, that's a bonus. Remember that somewhere out there is a hardworking salesman who needs and appreciates your help in finding sales prospects. His success is most important to the company's financial well-being.

6: Consumer Product Publicity

CONSUMER PRODUCT PUBLICITY is an economical and effective way to increase the sales of consumer products and to build a favorable public opinion of the company's brand name. With proper planning, management can use consumer product publicity as an effective part of a total marketing effort. This chapter is designed to develop and implement such planning.

THE ROLE OF CONSUMER PRODUCT PUBLICITY

Basically, the purpose of consumer product publicity is to obtain the highest degree of favorable response in all media and with the various publics for a particular company's products. When handled by public relations professionals who know tested publicity techniques, consumer publicity has a proven track record of helping build sales rapidly for new products. It also can find and promote new use patterns and stimulate new ideas for established patterns.

Product advertising through the purchase of media space or time is the conventional means of promoting sales. The product publicity effort, however, is aimed at securing so-called free space in media and other communications outlets. The assumption is that the product and the uses suggested by publicity are news and deserve coverage as such.

The techniques of consumer product publicity are many and varied. Some may be familiar, such as the press release, the media event mounted to introduce a new product, or scripts prepared on behalf of consumer product companies for use during the editorial portion of radio or television programs.

Other tools of the publicity trade are not as obvious and therefore not as easily understood. These include continuing contacts with editors, broadcasters, and trend setters on behalf of the consumer product company; the attendance of publicity professionals at sales meetings or key conventions; and even the carefully engineered in-store demonstrations of products, staged to exhibit product features that the professional has found to be of special interest to consumers.

Since product publicity encompasses so many areas, it is perhaps best to examine this function from the standpoint of what it can—and cannot—be expected to accomplish on behalf of a consumer product company.

SOME POSITIVES AND NEGATIVES

Consumer product publicity can—if the product is useful and valid—help a company's product become "news" to consumers. Many people read papers and magazines, watch television, or attend classes, workshops, or special events to find out what's new. Product publicity is the principal resource a company can use to answer that question, by providing information about a product that helps a person live better, cook faster, dress more fashionably or more comfortably, use leisure time in more creative ways, lighten the housekeeping load, or simply become more interested.

It is important to know that, although consumer publicity may obtain initial media attention for a product that is short on quality or innovation, it cannot sustain such attention very long. The most talented publicist cannot publicize mediocrity into success.

Consumer product publicity can supply the valuable implied endorsement of that product. This cloaks the product with a high degree of creditability. It puts the individual editors or broadcasters in a position of saying, in effect, that the product news is of sufficient interest and value that they wish to share it with their audience through their editorial columns or program time.

Although it is a common belief that connections are all-important, consumer publicity cannot be placed to any significant degree in the media simply because the professional "knows the editors." Publicity people, to be effective, seek a wide range of acquaintances within the media, but friendship alone won't get a lackluster product into print or trigger coverage on a radio or television broadcast.

Some of the positive features of consumer product publicity are discussed below.

Consumer product publicity can help a company reach many publics that are unreachable or unaffordable through other means. Few product advertising or direct mail budgets are large enough to enable a company to reach all consumers who are potential customers of a product. On the other hand, the ability of product publicity to reach a larger audience than advertising may be limited only by the degree of creativity involved in the publicity approach. Product publicity is a company's long-distance runner. When available advertising dollars must be redirected toward another product, publicity can continue to find new ways and new places to tell the product story.

Remember, however, that consumer publicity is not a substitute for advertising and merchandising. All parts of the marketing mix have their own functions. No matter how skilled they are, publicity people cannot guarantee exposure in the media at the times when a controlled, precisely timed message is absolutely essential for product sales, and in the markets where it is necessary.

Consumer product publicity usually costs less than advertising or the other components of a sophisticated marketing plan. A common misjudgment of management is the failure to budget sufficient funds for a publicity program. Consumer publicity is cost efficient, but it won't run on air. It requires and deserves a budget.

Consumer product publicity can supply an effective reconnaissance value. Those who manage the product publicity effort also have their own kinds of sales to make. To persuade communications outlets to accept and use news about the products, they must stress a wide variety of product advantages and uses. In most cases, advertising is not able to mention all such features within its normal limitations of space and money. Very often, extensive and frequent media pickup of a particular product advantage or use that is not emphasized in the product advertising can provide a signal to the sales force or advertising department and result in a revised strategy that underscores the consumer interest point that has been uncovered in the product publicity.

Although product publicity can serve a reconnaissance or exploratory function, it operates far less productively in a "rush-to-the-rescue" capacity. When publicity is used on a crash mission to build consumer attention and sales after all else fails, it will probably fail, too.

Consumer product publicity can help improve a company's image. Few corporate undertakings offer a clearer picture of a company than the visibility of its products as new. Not only what a company says about its products—and how, when, where, and by whom they are being used—but how the media present such information affects public assessment of a company's strength and worth.

Consumer product publicity can have a favorable influence on a number of secondary publics. The wide-ranging nature of publicity, in terms of media reach and exposure, can have a positive impact on many special publics that are important to a company. These may include the financial and investing public, the teaching community, wholesale and retail managements, legislative bodies monitoring corporate activities, and environmental action groups that keep an increasingly critical eye on what companies do, or don't do, to safeguard the nation's people and natural resources.

In summary, consumer product publicity is a highly effective marketing tool that can be used to great advantage by progressive management. It is not, contrary to lingering stereotypes, all stunts and press parties (even though both may be useful components of a total program) but rather a vital and efficient part of the sophisticated company's marketing mix.

A FRAMEWORK FOR CONSUMER PRODUCT
PUBLICITY PLANNING

In planning publicity programs, management should consider four steps. The first—explaining the marketing strategy—is a management responsibility. The next two—evaluating the product publicity plan and following the program through—are the responsibilities of the publicity staff or public relations agency. The final step—reporting and merchandising the successfully completed publicity effort—should be handled by both management and the publicity staff or agency. We shall discuss each of these steps in detail.

Explaining the Marketing Strategy

Management may want to meet with its publicity personnel in a separate session, or it may include them in the kickoff meeting at which all the divisions contributing to the introduction of a new product are present. Either way, the publicity representatives are there in a role much like that of reporters, seeking answers to these questions:

What is the product? What is it intended to do?

Is there a clear-cut market for the product?

Can the product's pricing, packaging, methods, and timetable for local, state, and national distribution be summarized?

Is the product truly new, or is it a refinement, adaptation, or improvement of a comparable product already on the market?

What is the principal product advantage? Are price, styling, and packaging subsidiary assets?

What contemporary living habits or consumer wants and needs will the product satisfy?

What are the sales goals for the product, both immediate and long range?

What product tests have been made that might provide copy strategy or feature slants in the publicity?

Does the product represent any kind of new departure for the company in terms of product development, entry into a new market, or price range in relation to other items carrying the company's brand name? Is the advertising and merchandising material complete and ready to go? What is the budget appropriation for this? What is the principal selling proposition or competitive difference to be emphasized in the advertising and merchandising thrust? Can the publicity personnel have copies of the advertising schedule? Are there subsidiary product advantages to emphasize that advertising may not be able to highlight in the introductory campaign?

How much time do product publicity personnel have to develop a program and a budget request?

The time limit set for delivery of a publicity plan and budget request can be flexible, but it is important that management has sufficient time to accept, reject, or modify the written proposal. This will give the publicity staff sufficient time so their start-up activity can coincide with the main marketing objectives.

Evaluating the Product Publicity Plan

Obviously, there is no standard length for a publicity plan. The marketing manager's evaluation should assess the plan on how well it describes and supports these principal elements:

1. Recommended event or activities designed to present the initial and persuasive product introduction to the press.

2. Activities planned to assure news or feature coverage in the major media: newspapers, magazines, radio and television, wire services, special feature syndicates and writers, and trade and professional press.

3. Recommendations for special publicity or educational materials developed for schools, service clubs, or consumer groups or to take advantage of seasonal or special events.

4. Publicity efforts aimed to reach the important secondary publics that provide consumers and also influence product attention and acceptance: the educational community, the financial commu-

nity, the company's own employee audience, the advertising press, company suppliers, and so on.

5. Recommendations for any new descriptive brochures or audiovisual treatment of the product that could broaden the size of the consumer audience.

6. Recommended budget for the consumer product publicity program, generally presented in two sections. The first section covers the estimated month-by-month operating costs of the publicity program, including such expenses as those for photography, printing of releases, outside consultants or specialists, and travel. The second section usually lists nonrecurring expenses, such as the costs of a press party introduction, special literature or film, and travel of a company publicity representative to major market cities for media interviews and appearances.

Following the Publicity Program Through

The effectiveness of product publicity as a marketing program component can best be described in an actual case history of a company that understands the potentials and limitations of this communications technique. The program for Wear-Ever Aluminum, Inc., a leading manufacturer of kitchen equipment and appliances, demonstrates the versatility and product sales influence that a well-conceived and -executed product publicity plan can have. The program has reached millions of readers and listeners in a wide range of publics and has resulted in an astonishing sales success for the Wear-Ever® Super Shooter electric foodgun.

For more than a half-century, Wear-Ever had specialized, almost exclusively, in the manufacture and sales of quality cookware and bakeware. A few years ago, the company made the decision to begin manufacturing and marketing a new line of specialty cookware products. As its first product, the company designed an electric cookie, canape, and candy "gun," with immediate "fire away" food preparation possibilities. They named it the "Super Shooter." The product brought a new convenience to the kitchen.

The company realized that the introduction of this new product would require supplying a considerable amount of information to the consumers. In addition to advertising the new product, Wear-Ever strengthened two aspects of its national marketing program. First, it increased the number of in-store demonstration personnel, so that more potential consumers could witness the in-use values of this unfamiliar product in several thousand retail outlets that stocked the Wear-Ever line. Second, it involved its publicity staff in the formative stages of the product introduction planning and incorporated that staff into a full working partnership in the new-product venture. A shortened chronicle of the product publicity efforts and the results follows.

Because of the natural link between the Super Shooter and holiday entertaining, Wear-Ever decided to introduce its product to the media before the Christmas season. The location for the press party—complete with trimmed Christmas trees, pine garlands, and chamber music—was New York City.

The event drew a large number of editors and reporters from wire services and syndicates, the major consumer interest magazines, metropolitan papers, and broadcast media. Magazine stories generated by the in-action demonstration of the Super Shooter at the press party reached a total of 52 million readers. Daily newspaper coverage added another 64 million. Trade publications, whose interest was vital to Wear-Ever in terms of building dealer interest in the product, brought news of Wear-Ever's product and promotional support to another 2 million retailing and wholesaler subscribers.

When the new product was introduced at the largest trade show in the world—the January exposition of the National Housewares Manufacturers Association in Chicago—Wear-Ever was already cashing in on its national marketing effort. Working out of the company's display area on the floor of Chicago's mammoth convention center, McCormick Place, the company's product publicity specialists were able to interest television networks covering the show to feature the foodgun as one of the most imaginative items of the 10,000 new housewares and appliance products exhibited that week.

Shortly after the debut of the Super Shooter at the Chicago exposition, Wear-Ever hired a freelance home economist to demonstrate and talk about the Super Shooter on television and radio programs, in newspaper interviews, and in some of the company's major retail outlets. While this 33-city tour was in progress, the company and its public relations agency completed two booklets about the product.

The first of these was a 30-page, two-color recipe booklet, "The Super Shooter Idea Book," which was given to every Super Shooter purchaser. Shortly thereafter, Wear-Ever completed another piece of how-to-use literature, "The Ready Aim Cookbook," which was offered for sale in bookstores and housewares departments of retail stores. While these developments were taking place, feature stories and photographs detailing new-use ideas for the Super Shooter continued to be released and subsequently published by newspapers around the country.

Total outlay for the national program of product publicity was only slightly more than the amount charged by one New York television station for one minute of commercial advertising time.

One year after the first Super Shooter came off the line, and with extra factory shifts turning out the product to meet consumer demand, Wear-Ever stopped production just long enough to lift a completed Super Shooter from the assembly line. That particular Super Shooter was mounted on a plaque and presented to the product publicity specialist who had participated in the first strategy sessions and who had suggested the name for the new product. The gift was the one-millionth electric foodgun to be manufactured at Wear-Ever's main plant and headquarters at Chillicothe, Ohio.

Wear-Ever has since introduced other specialty products in addition to the Super Shooter. However, the company continues to use aggressive product publicity to build sales for the premier product of the line. A five-minute film entitled "An Entertaining Lifestyle," which positions the Super Shooter as a major contributor to specialty recipe preparation in the home, has been shown on more than 200 local television stations, reaching an estimated 6 million viewers during the editorial portion of TV programming. On the second Christmas anniversary of the product, another 80 television stations received the foodgun along with a recipe for a Christmas cookie. Magazine editors continue to visit the test kitchens of Wear-Ever's public relations agency in New York City to discuss the incorporation of the product in their own seasonal features, and Wear-Ever continues to mail newspapers a quarterly series of food photographs featuring the Super Shooter in new-use applications. One of these mailings, based on Valentine's Day candy and cookie recipes, was used by newspapers reaching 9.5 million readers.

The company's sales success with the product and the consumer press attention that the product receives has been noted by influential publications. *The New York Times, The Wall Street Journal,* and *Home Furnishings Daily* have reported at length on the risk that Wear-Ever assumed in moving out of a comfortable marketing position into a dynamic product leadership role.

During an interview the company's public relations director, Robert Vogt, told us that product publicity was an influential factor in Wear-Ever's assumption of a leadership role in the specialty housewares industry. "Publicity gave us a direct line to consumers when these important potential purchasers were most receptive to news about an innovative and useful new product. And now that many of these people are Super Shooter owners, publicity keeps them 'sold' on the value of our product," he said.

Reporting and Merchandising the Results

The alert company will use two principal channels to merchandise the results of successful product publicity activity. One of these is the trade and business news press. The second is the channel the company itself has formed to keep its own internal publics—sales force, stockholders, store demonstrators, and employees—informed of the impact that product publicity has on the consumer public and the media. Direct mail, the annual and quarterly reports, bulletin boards, and stories in company house organs are all ways to communicate the news that can build and retain confidence and pride in a company and its marketing ability. Product publicity relies on all these outlets to disseminate its successful results.

SUPERVISING PRODUCT PUBLICITY: A CHECKLIST FOR MANAGEMENT

Each program of product publicity must be shaped by the product to be publicized. However, management can look to a basic checklist for help in structuring its relationship with the publicity staff or agency. The principal rules that apply across the board to the managers of product publicity are:

1. Include product publicity personnel at the beginning of the marketing strategy sessions.

2. Give your publicity people a thorough briefing of what the product is, what it is expected to do, and how well it is expected to perform. They, in turn, should give you a detailed plan and budget, covering anticipated activity and results.

3. Allow some elbow room for creativity in writing for and contact with media within the formal limits of the publicity plan. Almost every consumer product has the potential for unanticipated and valuable editorial treatment—"opportunity targets" that may take shape when an editor wishes to link your product with an emerging living pattern or trend.

4. Make certain the proposed publicity plan covers all available publics—internal as well as external—that are not covered by other marketing budget appropriations.

5. Be prepared to live with the limitations as well as the strengths of product publicity. Advertising appears the way you want it to appear and when you want it to appear. The consumer publicity effort is dependent on the media and is not as controllable as advertising.

6. Merchandise the good news that is developed by product publicity. It's an effective way to keep morale high and product quality on target.

7. Finally, recognize that consumer product publicity has the capability to build sales for new products and stimulate new-use patterns and ideas.

7: Employee Communications

FOR MANY YEARS the function known as employee or internal communications seemed to languish in most organizations as a task of relatively little importance. Some viewed it as a nice-to-have extra but certainly not a necessity. Others saw it as a burdensome requirement of questionable value. To a large extent, those days are gone. During the 1970s, the employee communications function emerged as a strong growth area of public relations activity.

EMERGENCE OF EMPLOYEE COMMUNICATIONS FUNCTION

According to the International Association of Business Communicators (IABC), the largest professional organization in the field, the current recognition of internal communications as an important and valuable function of management is evidenced by a recent surge in newly created positions, higher salaries, broader responsibilities, more formalized communications programs, and the creation of separate internal communications departments in many organizations.

In the past, employee communications was frequently a stepchild of the personnel or public relations department. It tended to be second- or third-priority work, often relegated to people who were thought to be incapable of handling anything really important. Even in organizations where the employee communications function was taken more seriously, it still took a back seat to "more important" personnel work or communications with customers, dealers, shareholders, and other publics.

Today, thousands of well-educated communications professionals are involved in planning policy and strategy and in executing a
wide range of activities and programs inside corporations, financial
institutions, associations, educational institutions, hospitals, and
government agencies. They use a variety of media—ranging from
bulletin boards to telephone hotlines—to communicate with large
and small internal audiences. Their subjects, too, have changed
dramatically. They now include worker satisfaction, job enrich-
ment, economics, government regulation, compensation, benefits,
social responsibility and accountability, foreign competition, con-
sumerism, environmentalism, and labor relations.

Based on its tremendous growth and evolution during the 1970s,
employee communications will almost certainly continue to increase in importance and stature during the 1980s.

Sophisticated organizations now recognize employee communications as a true management function. They understand the employees of today and realize that the key to any organization's
success is its people. They are aware that effective employee communications can pay off in positive morale, high standards of work
quality and productivity, pride in the company and its products or
services, lower absenteeism, and workforce stability.

Nonetheless, in many, less aware organizations employee communications continues to be a low-priority activity. Perhaps the
responsibility is treated superficially with a poor-quality company
publication laden with bowling scores, big-fish photographs, and
profound proclamations from the boss. The management of such
organizations apparently fails to realize that some type of communication to and among employees does indeed occur continuously, whether or not management chooses to direct the process
and use it as a tool.

The philosophical approach any organization adopts toward
employee communications is usually a direct result of the attitudes
of its top management concerning all types of communications and
of those placed in charge of the function. If management tends to

view employees impersonally, then those who have the responsibility for employee communications will usually view the function as a task of marginal importance. Employee communications in such organizations will be infrequent, inconsistent, and ineffective.

More enlightened managements, however, recognize the bottom-line value of treating people as people, of communicating with them about the goals, activities, and problems of the organization from which they derive their livelihood. This more informed approach to employee communications is reflected in the statement of a chief executive who told an interviewer: "The best business plan is meaningless unless everyone is aware of it and pulling together to achieve its objectives. Good communications are the lifeblood of any enterprise, large or small. Communications are essential to keep our entire organization functioning at maximum levels and to make the most of our greatest management resource—our people."

The recent growth of employee communications activity stems in large part from the social changes and shifting attitudes our entire society has experienced since the 1960s. These have included increased concern for self as opposed to the old-fashioned work ethic based on self-denial; unprecedented acceptance of pluralism and diversity in the areas of race, sex, and religion; the changing role of women; and the rising sense of entitlement.

Workers who have grown up with these changing societal values virtually demand a more sophisticated, sensitive approach to employee communications. Today's employees exhibit characteristics that are significantly different from those of the past. They tend to be less money oriented and more driven by a desire for personal fulfillment. They need more frequent and more detailed direct feedback on their work performance than did their fathers and mothers. They want to be seen and acknowledged. Today's workers are eager for a sense of participation. They want to be "in the know" and to be asked for their opinions. More precisely, they expect the people who run the organizations they work for to treat them as people, not as numbers. They want information, not orders.

Another important catalyst in the growth of employee communications activity has been the government. Some recent legislation, particularly in the areas of safety and retirement programs, has actually mandated more and better communications with employees. In addition, the growth of government regulation and its direct involvement in business operations has prompted many companies to increase their employee communications activities in an effort to tell their side of the story and to generate support and understanding among employees. The result has been a tremendous increase in economic education programs and the creation of political action committees, with their attendant communications activities.

DEVELOPING A PROGRAM

Any person who has responsibility for employee communications faces a complex and difficult challenge. The primary task is to create and maintain a climate of trust and credibility within the organization. The only sure way to do this is to communicate candidly about the subjects that affect the organization and concern the employees. Obviously, this includes providing adequate means for upward as well as downward communication. Openness and honesty in employee communications cannot be turned on and off to suit the occasion or the subject. They must be the rule, not the exception.

Assuming that the management of your organization recognizes the vital importance of good employee communications and assuming it has a commitment to honesty and openness, what should you do if you are given responsibility for the internal communications function?

First, conduct an audit of all the internal communications activities that are going on throughout your organization. This can be a fairly simple review that involves talking to a few knowledgeable people in the organization and collecting samples of all company publications. Or it can be a more formalized audit, perhaps even involving the use of an outside counseling firm. The latter approach might be advisable if you do not feel qualified to evaluate publications or other forms of communication from a professional or technical standpoint.

The objective of the audit, regardless of how you decide to do it, should be to identify, quantify, and evaluate the existing employee communications effort. This should include the types of messages that are being conveyed, the target audiences at which they are directed, and the various media that are being used.

Next, take a close, critical look at the people who are currently doing the communications work. Through personal interviews and discussions with people at various levels of the organization, try to determine whether or not the communicators are actually helping to build an atmosphere of trust and credibility. Are they regarded as capable professionals, or are they viewed condescendingly as less than competent? Do they get on well with others in the organization, or are they viewed as cynical, negative people?

These two initial steps—auditing the existing effort and reviewing the people—are vital even if your organization has previously had little or no formal employee communications effort. Communication among employees is always going on; there is never a complete information void. Employees find out about management and organizational changes; they learn about labor problems and plant closings at other locations. They somehow become aware of countless other things, good and bad, that go on within the organization. They may find out late and then may get wrong or incomplete information, but communication of some sort does take place.

After you know specifically what is—or is not—being done and you have some understanding of how well the people involved are doing it, you can then determine with some degree of confidence where improvements and changes are most needed.

Setting the Objectives

Your next step is to set realistic, achievable objectives for an internal communications program. This is best done as part of the overall strategic planning for the total organization, taking into account the goals of management and the real-world limitations, such as budget and staffing restrictions, under which it must operate. Make your objectives as specific as possible; if they are too broad and all-encompassing, they are meaningless.

The objectives must be considered separately from the techniques and media that might be employed to achieve them. For example, the nature of your business and the size of your organization may make it difficult for employees to receive news about company activities in a timely manner. If it is important that they have access to such news, then you might establish an objective to supply employees at all locations with timely access to news that affects the organization. To help meet that objective, you might choose a technique such as setting up a telephone news service, developing a weekly videotape program, or publishing a daily compendium of news clippings.

Many organizations prepare long- and short-range objectives for their internal communications efforts. Such statements can serve as a charter for the communications function itself and as guidelines for those who work in the field on a day-to-day basis. The fundamental objective of any internal communications program, of course, is to help the organization achieve the purposes for which it was created—whether it is a business, a hospital, a university, or a trade association.

In formulating your communications objectives, you should consider not only the needs and desires of the organization and its management but also the concerns and desires of the employees. Mutual understanding is a key to successful, effective communication. Surveys conducted over the past several years have detected significant changes in the kinds of subjects that are of interest and concern to employees. In general, the thrust of these changes has been away from personal chitchat toward more meaty topics, such as changes in company policies and benefits programs and messages from management about the organization's future, the competition, and the economic outlook.

An important step in establishing objectives and then planning your communications activities is to clearly define your target audiences. Analyze the employee population of your organization in terms of location, type of activity, and such demographics as age, sex, education level, and length of time with the company. Typical audiences might include such groups as the top management team, a broader-based key management group, long-term salaried employees, inside and field sales forces, production supervisors, hourly employees, union leadership, and technical professionals. Learning about the size and makeup of each important segment within your overall employee population will help you establish communications objectives for each target group.

Once you have audited the existing communications efforts, evaluated the effectiveness of the communicators, analyzed your employee population, and formulated objectives based on the organization's goals and the employees' concerns, you have laid the foundation for an internal communications program. Now you are ready to consider the more tangible aspects of internal communications, the media.

Selecting the Media

Some channels and methods of communication are traditionally identified with employee communications, for example, the company newspaper and bulletin boards. In recent years, however, there has been a very marked trend toward the use of many different types of media for employee communications. The traditional company newspaper is still there and so is the bulletin board, but they are now just part of an internal media mix that also includes videotaped closed-circuit television, slides, newsletters, posters, exhibits, telephone information hotlines, face-to-face meetings, and family-day open houses.

Another major development is the new emphasis on two-way

communication. Recently there has been a significant increase in the use of upward communications techniques such as feedback programs, management–employee meetings, and readership and attitude surveys.

In evaluating and selecting media to be used in an internal communications program, primary consideration must be given to your objectives and to the budget you have available. Perhaps you cannot afford videotape programs and telephone hotlines, but neither can you afford to ignore the need for communicating within your organization as effectively as your resources will allow. Here is a checklist of some employee communications media and techniques that many organizations use in one form or another.

Employee Publications. For most organizations, some type of regularly issued publication is the backbone of the internal communications program. The type of publication that is best for your situation may be a black-and-white monthly newspaper, a typewritten weekly newsletter, or a full-color quarterly magazine. For large, complex organizations, more than one publication is usually necessary to report on policies and operations and to cover the activities and subjects that are of interest to employees in various parts of the organization. Depending on your objectives and the various target audiences within your organization, you may need a combination of a quarterly management newsletter and several divisional publications. Whatever types of publications are required, issuing them on a regular basis in a consistent format is essential. If your budget allows, it is usually better to mail the publication to employees' homes in order to achieve increased readership among family members.

Videotape. One of the newest and probably most effective media available for employee communication is videotape. Obviously it is more expensive than some other forms of communication, but its reach, impact, and effectiveness with today's visually oriented employees make it well worth the investment for many organizations. Videotape programs of extremely good quality are being produced for a variety of purposes: to acquaint newly hired people with their organization, to train employees, to make them aware of new products and facilities, and to inform them about new customer reaction to products and about research projects. In some organizations videotape programs are supplanting the traditional publication as the basic internal communications tool.

Surveys. Two types of surveys are used most frequently for employee communications purposes—attitude surveys and readership surveys. The former are used to ascertain employees' attitudes and perceptions regarding company policies, work practices, management techniques, salary and benefits programs, communications practices, and various other issues relating to how the organization deals with its people. Such surveys can be invaluable in detecting potential problems early and in measuring the employees' understanding of company practices and programs. Readership surveys are conducted specifically to measure the degree of reader interest in the various subjects that are covered in a publication and to gauge the overall reaction of readers to the publication. If properly executed, such surveys can be of tremendous value in determining the effectiveness of your publications and in planning ways to make them better. The use of surveys clearly indicates to employees that management is interested in their opinions. However, surveys also raise employees' expectations for change and improvement, so they should not be undertaken unless management is willing to make changes based on what it learns.

Slide and Tape Presentations. This versatile medium, which combines 35-mm slides and audiotape, can be adapted for a variety of purposes and is frequently used for explaining salary and benefits programs and for new-employee orientation. Slides can include both printed copy and artwork or photographs as well as charts and graphs. The narration is usually recorded with appropriate background music and sound effects. Inaudible electronic impulses are placed on the tape to automatically change the slides at the proper points in the presentation.

Meetings. Properly planned and orchestrated meetings can be a valuable method of communicating with various audiences about goals and progress, of seeking solutions to specific problems, and of discussing matters of common concern. The use of meetings for employee communications purposes should be carefully considered, from top management staff meetings, through large gatherings of people, to small informal briefing sessions for front-line supervisors. Many companies are now using meetings between management and small groups of employees as part of their feedback programs. Meetings with employees, individually and in small groups, are also used effectively to reinforce written communications on complicated or unpleasant topics such as plant closings or layoffs.

Annual Report. Some organizations prepare special annual reports for employees or send their regular annual report to employees with a letter from management. This can be an excellent way of interpreting the past year's performance and financial results for employees and for positioning the challenges of the coming year. The formats of annual reports for employees range from simple folders to elaborate magazines. Some companies simply produce a special issue or section of their regular employee publication to serve as their annual report to employees.

Daily News Digest. Some organizations publish a daily digest of selected news items that have appeared in general circulation newspapers, trade magazines, and other publications. This is frequently a single sheet prepared each morning and distributed to employees and posted on bulletin boards during the noon hour. Such publications are an effective way of keeping employees informed about matters of immediate interest and concern. Weekly or monthly digests are also good vehicles.

Bulletin Boards. Someone once said the world is divided into two kinds of people—those who always read bulletin boards and those who never do. Despite the fact that a certain portion of the employee audience does not look at bulletin boards, this age-old medium is nonetheless of significant value for communicating important, brief items quickly. Two things that discourage people from reading bulletin boards regularly are leaving items on the board too long and posting multipage notices that take too much time to read. Give some commonsense consideration to where the bulletin boards are located, and assign someone the responsibility of approving items to be posted and removing notices after they have been up for a specified period of time.

Letters to Employees' Homes. For subjects of particular importance, it is not unusual for key executives to send letters directly to their employees at home. This can be particularly valuable for communicating information that is of interest to employees' families, such as details about new work practices, changes in employee relations practices or benefits, or recognition for special achievements. This medium should be reserved for subjects of special importance to maintain the considerable positive impact a personal letter from the boss can have.

Employee Manual. Detailed descriptions and explanations of benefits and pension plans are now required by law for many organizations. In addition, many companies find it helpful to publish manuals containing statements of basic company policies, rules of work, and miscellaneous information about the company's history, products, and facilities. Such manuals are frequently furnished to new employees as part of a comprehensive orientation program.

Special Events. Company-sponsored events, such as family-day open houses, summer picnics, Christmas parties, and group outings to sports events, are used to develop a sense of belonging to the company family and to create esprit de corps. Employee committees are usually set up to plan and carry out these events under the guidance of the personnel department.

Organized Activities. Closely related to special events are company-sponsored activities such as sports teams, travel clubs, contests, involvement in Junior Achievement and other organizations, and participation in United Way campaigns and other community activities. Obviously, such activities overlap with community relations efforts, but they have significant employee communications value in many organizations.

In-Plant Exhibits. Exhibits featuring products and showing photographs of people involved in various types of work are frequently used in connection with employee recognition efforts, the introduction of new products or facilities, and an organization's health, safety, and educational programs.

Additional examples of media that could be used for employee communications include posters, company films, local advertising, employee activities committees and management clubs, and combination incentive/communications programs designed to increase productivity.

The effective use of any of these media requires considerable technical skill. Determining the objectives and strategy for their effective use requires considerable management skill.

Employee communications in the 1980s can be one of the most exciting and gratifying areas of the public relations field, or it can be dull and frustrating. The difference lies in how the function is perceived by those who manage the organization. Part of the employee communications challenge continues to be educating top management about the importance of communicating with employees. The key question is: Do the top executives of your organization view internal communications as a tool and responsibility of management or as an unnecessary luxury?

Remember, however, that even a well-executed internal communications program based on sound objectives cannot ensure the overall success of an organization any more than any other single program or function can. Employee communications must be kept in the proper perspective as just one important element in the overall management of the organization. If your products are not competitive, if your financial situation is unstable, if your manufacturing facilities are hopelessly inefficient, good employee communications is not going to keep you in business.

8: Financial Communications

FEW FUNCTIONS that come under the broad umbrella of public relations cause as much misunderstanding—and in some cases trepidation—as financial communications. The word *financial,* implying involvement of large sums of money, may be intimidating. The thought that Big Brother—that is, the Securities and Exchange Commission—is watching may cause apprehension. Perhaps anything that is labeled "financial" may sound too esoteric to those who are not professionals in the field.

Take heart. When you are assigned to manage this special public relations function for the first time, you'll find that what you already know will go a long way in helping you master the new responsibility.

IT'S DIFFERENT, BUT IT ISN'T

To help you get on top of the subject, here's a good definition of financial communications:

> Financial communications is the discipline under which information about a publicly held company is released through public channels to all those who need the information to form an opinion on the investment merit of the company.

It is hoped that this definition will lessen emphasis on the word *financial* and place the emphasis where it belongs, on the word *communications.* This is a communicating function whose subject happens to be financial. You must be a good communicator to

95

manage it properly. Unfamiliarity with the subject matter, which can be learned, should not hinder anyone who is already a good communicator.

The same basic rules apply here as to any other public relations function involving preparation of information and its release to selected audiences. Information must be released in a form immediately useful to editors; it must be in language that is readily understood by editors and their readers; it must be released promptly; and it must be properly directed to the audiences for which it is intended.

But there are differences to be kept in mind.

Accuracy

Accuracy, important in any communications effort, is essential here because you are transmitting information that will have immediate impact on investment decisions involving thousands of individuals and, possibly, millions of dollars. An error in words or figures can cause such severe damage that a later retraction or correction may not be able to rectify it. You may be embarrassed in announcing, for example, that a new product will not be in the stores until September when your press release originally said August. However, you will be not just embarrassed but in real trouble if a decimal point in a company's earnings statement is in the wrong place or if the chairman's message about the company's prospects has been garbled.

So, proofread, then proofread again, and then again—preferably with some sharp-eyed person who can read the original, approved version to you while you check it against what you're sending out.

Subject to Regulations

Not even old pros with years of experience are ever quite sure what the SEC means (or wants) in its regulations. Trends in regulations tend to change with the personalities of succeeding SEC commissioners and the goals of new administrations. Still, you must be up to date on Washington's latest rules for "protecting" the American investor.

Some of these rules suggest that the investor (the individual investor, at least) is as close to extinction as the snail darter. There is great concern about the investor's ability to look after himself. To prevent trouble with the SEC, not to mention investors themselves, avoid:

o Any implication of impropriety on the part of the company or its executives.
o Withholding news from the general public, thereby enabling insiders to have access to it and act on it first.
o Misleading information or any statement not based on fact.
o Projections about future developments that could be wide of the mark.

Immediate Release

The financial communications practitioner does not have the luxury of timing release of information to coincide with some public event that will heighten interest in the news. The moment the news is born, whether results for a financial reporting period or a development that will have impact on the company's future, it must be released immediately. There are good times and bad times to release financial news (more on this later), but often you do not have an option. If the development that you are reporting is final and the wire services have not yet closed down for the night, you must release it at once. Sitting on news of crucial importance for financial audiences is asking for trouble.

Long-Term Effort

Financial communications, perhaps more than any other public relations function, requires patience and a long-term viewpoint. Each step in the program is like adding a brick to a house that is being built to withstand any storm that may come along in the future. Don't seek short-term impact by inflating language or information; this may turn against you over the long term.

If you keep in mind the requirements of absolute accuracy, compliance with SEC regulations, and the need for immediate disclosure of pertinent information, your previous public relations experience, or even previous business experience if you have not handled public relations before, can be readily applied to the financial communications function. To master the subject, though, you must have a good fix on some special considerations.

DEFINING YOUR AUDIENCES

There are well-defined, special audiences in financial communications. This is no more unusual than the fact that a story about jogging should be sent to the media that are read or viewed by people who jog.

Investment Professionals

The broad term *investment professionals* includes all those involved in any aspect of buying or selling securities as part of their professional function. In other words, it includes everybody whose actions or opinions are related to investment decisions. The list includes:

o Security analysts who study certain companies and make periodic recommendations as to whether their stocks should be bought, sold, or held.

o Portfolio managers who are responsible for investment vehicles such as bank trust accounts, pension funds, and mutual funds.

o Financial counselors who make a living telling other people what to buy and sell.

o People who work for the so-called institutions (banks, mutual funds, insurance companies, etc.), those who work for brokerage houses, and possibly, retail brokers. (When and how you might include brokerage salespeople as part of your audience is discussed later on.)

What does the investment professional (from here on let's call him the IP) want to hear and what does he need to know? This varies, of course, with how interested he is in your company. The degree of his interest can best be determined by direct contact. Ask him. General principles, however, can be helpful as guidelines.

The IP, assuming that he does follow your company, is less interested in what has happened than in what is likely to happen. If he follows your company, he already knows a lot about it. If he is only beginning to follow the company, a little research can bring him up to date. He wants your financial communications program to tell him how your company is doing on a quarter-by-quarter basis and how to interpret what is happening or might happen in terms of the future.

Here a word of caution. The relationship of the IP to the company is not unlike that of a reporter to his news source. The reporter's job is to find out all he can; the news source may want to tell only part of what the reporter seeks. The financial communications program should be geared to telling the inquiring IP as much as possible within reasonable limits set by company policy and competitive considerations.

There is one basic rule that you should never break and that an IP should not ask you to break: That is the prohibition against giving any individual, or group of individuals, new-material information that has not yet been made public. Nobody should have exclusive use, even for a short period of time, of important information that could affect investment opinion about the company. If you ever inadvertently spill the beans, you should immediately make the information generally known through a press release.

There are several ways to keep the investment community informed on a regular basis in a manner that does not compromise the company's interests or violate SEC regulations governing disclosure.

MAILINGS

The basic requirement for a successful mailing program is a complete and accurate mailing list. Unfortunately, because of frequent job changes in the investment community, no list will be absolutely correct at any given time. But an effort must be made to keep your list up to date.

The Financial Analysts Federation's annual directory is one way to find out who is doing what, and where. Also, a number of firms specialize in preparing lists of investment people who cover your industry, if not your company. But it is wise not to rely completely on lists that can never be 100 percent accurate.

Assuming you have sufficient time and staff, making your own telephone calls to key people at institutions and brokerage houses is the best way to make sure who should be on the company's financial mailing list. During tempestuous times in the securities industry, when mergers and internal shake-ups are rife, some individuals seem simply to disappear. But the chances are most of these people will surface in a similar job in another firm. Always conduct a mailing survey at least once a year to determine if your list is accurate. Enclose a self-addressed, stamped reply card and ask each person to indicate whether he wishes to continue to receive your mailings and also if the affiliation you have for him is correct.

MEETINGS

Most IPs appreciate an opportunity to meet with corporate management. Although they prefer talking with top management, most are happy to meet with the company's financial spokesperson, usually the director of investor relations, for regular updating of their information on the company. Either public or private meetings can be held for this purpose.

A public meeting is an appearance before any of the 48 member societies of the Financial Analysts Federation. A presentation to any one of these societies can have a favorable impact on the national investment community. But you have to be invited. If your company is large and well known, you probably will receive an invitation from several of these member societies. If you are less well known, you may have to ask for an invitation. You may not get one, however, because of your size or because of lack of current interest in your industry. We suggest you request an invitation from the program chairman of the society in a city in which you'd like to appear. Send him background material on the company with your request, so he can make a case for you before his committee. If you're turned down, be patient and try again later. Public appearances at analysts societies meetings have important advantages. They give you immediate access to a cross-section of the local community. Because the meeting is public, you will probably get coverage in the local press and possibly in the national edition of *The Wall Street Journal.*

Even if you are invited to appear before societies, do not neglect the private meeting. Actually, there are two kinds of private meetings—the purely private and the semiprivate—and both have their advantages and disadvantages.

The purely private meeting is the one you set up entirely on your own. You determine the guest list, time, place, and content of your presentation; issue the invitations; and prepare the menu. The advantage is that you control the entire meeting. You come into town as an independent visitor, not linked to any local firm or institution. By avoiding "linkage," you will not turn off some important people in firms that are competitors of the sponsoring firm or individual.

With a semiprivate meeting, you are sponsored by a local firm that usually makes all the arrangements. This obviously is easier, since all you have to do is show up and give the presentation. But local sponsorship may give an impression that you are somehow in the sponsor's pocket. You are usually better off setting up your own meeting.

Some firms are, so to speak, in the meeting business. For a fee, which may be in the form of a charge for some collateral service, these firms will invite you to appear before an audience they select, an audience that they usually claim to be a blue ribbon group that no one else could get together for you. Such claims should be viewed with skepticism. However, sponsorship by reliable firms in this field can be helpful if you do not have the time or the staff to set up something yourself.*

---

* For a detailed account of how to set up meetings with investment professionals throughout the United States, see W. H. Friedman, "Winning West of the Hudson," *Public Relations Quarterly* (Spring 1978).

Shareholders

Cultivating relationships with individual shareholders in these days of capital shortages and capital formation problems is extremely important. So much so that most companies set up an independent shareholder relations office, which may or may not come under the financial communications function. If communication with shareholders does come within your managerial responsibility, the basic techniques and tools will be the same for this audience as for the IPs, but the approach will be somewhat different.

Most shareholders obtain the information they need and want through the annual and interim reports, proxy statements, and other materials mailed out by the company during the course of the year. The annual meeting, of course, is when management meets face to face with shareholders. The trend of holding these meetings in different cities each year has given more shareholders an opportunity to attend and to increase their sense of participation in company affairs.

Most individual shareholders do not seek the in-depth information that IPs require. Nor do they seek meetings with management more often than once a year. Routine mailings usually suffice to keep the shareholders aware of company progress. However, one communication that some companies direct to new shareholders is highly recommended—the welcoming letter. A short, friendly message from the chief executive officer of the company to new shareholders gives them the feeling that they are more than just names and numbers on the shareholder list. In an era of hostile takeover attempts, the welcoming letter may strengthen shareholder loyalty to management.

Other Audiences

Although they are technically in the IP group, retail brokers, or registered representatives, as they are often called, are not as important an audience as the research, money management, and counseling sectors of the IP fraternity. Many brokers, though, do make their own recommendations to their customers. They seek and are influenced by information supplied directly to them by corporations. In some cities, brokers have set up their own luncheon societies that invite corporate managements to make presentations. Many brokers are happy to attend special private meetings set up for the sales staff by companies seeking broader stock distribution.

Direct broker contact, however, may have little impact. Most brokers are required to recommend stocks covered by the firm's research department. Any recommendations outside the approved group usually must be justified to the office manager, and there is a trend toward stricter supervision over what brokers recommend. This is a result of lawsuits brokerage houses have faced from irate customers claiming that their accounts were mishandled or that they lost money because of questionable recommendations by the firm.

Other minor audiences that deserve some consideration are corporate suppliers, civic leaders, and any others who may have contact with the company and can be considered potential investors.

CREDIBILITY

Your audiences have now been defined. Your general knowledge of public relations techniques has been refined to meet the special requirements of financial communications. Now you are ready to explore the responsibilities involved in the management of the program. First, you must understand your basic objective in getting the corporate story across to these audiences. This is, quite simply, to establish and maintain corporate credibility.

With so much competition for investors' attention, it is much easier to turn off an audience than it is to turn it on. If you are inconsistent in what you say and do, you'll probably lose the best part of your audience. A false or overly optimistic statement or a confusing change in direction can take years to remedy.

Consider the case of a retail chain that some years ago got carried away with its prospects. Management in a presentation before a major analysts society flatly predicted earnings that failed, by a wide margin, to materialize. For a long time, Wall Street ignored the company because it did not believe what the company said. With the help of outside counsel, the firm went to work to win back its audience. Almost five years of consistent, realistic financial communications were needed before the company regained its following.

Credibility is fragile. It takes a long time to establish, but it can be destroyed overnight. You must establish and maintain credibility in an environment that definitely does not like companies that have to say they're sorry. Here's how:

1. Promptly disclose major corporate developments as they happen, in a manner that will reach the investing public as quickly as possible.
2. Maintain regular contact with the investment community through published materials and meetings held at regular intervals.
3. Be accessible for inquiries from IPs and give fair answers to fair questions. If you cannot answer, give a valid reason why you cannot.
4. Use one, and only one, company financial spokesman for ongoing and long-term contact with the investment community.
5. Be as frank as you can without harming company interests.

BEYOND MEASURE

The manager who likes to plot results of a program on a chart, nice and neat, will be frustrated by financial communications. Public relations activities are difficult to measure at best. Meaningful month-by-month or quarter-by-quarter measurement is virtually impossible in the financial area, where the results you seek are long term and the marketplace is capricious and uncertain.

Beware of trying to gauge the program's success in terms of the price of the stock, or the number of new shareholders recorded in a given period of time, or the number of reports investment companies have written on the company during the reference period.

And beware of management's asking you to justify the program in these terms.

The price of a company's stock and the amount of attention the company gets from the investment community will be determined by the company's performance and the judgment of the marketplace. Your mission is to make sure that the marketplace has all the information it needs to make an intelligent judgment about the company and about the investment merit of its stock. If you are telling the story properly to the right people, you should be able to look back and see genuine progress over the longer run in terms of stock price and investment interest. Don't paint yourself into a corner by setting specific short-term goals or letting management set them for you.

One large corporation had an unenthusiastic following in the investment community. Furthermore, very few people in that community understood the company or its goals. A financial communications program was set up to develop more frequent and more informative meetings with IPs, improve corporate literature, and assure greater accessibility of management. The situation has completely changed and the company is now regarded as one of the best and most reliable communicators in its industry—but the turn-around took 10 years. In other words, you must have patience.

Patience, however, does not mean inactivity. Success requires an active program that makes use of various public relations techniques, most of them probably already familiar to you.

BREAKING INTO PRINT

A financial communications program, like most other public relations activities, relies heavily on the media, specifically the print media and, within that category, the financial press.

Working with the Press

The press release is the basic vehicle for fast-breaking developments involving such events as interim or annual results, major acquisitions, and changes in top management. The news must be distributed immediately to channels that will deliver the information to the maximum number of people as quickly as possible. This means getting the story to a wire service, above all to the Dow Jones broad tape, which is the broadest-based news service reaching the financial community. If your story appears on the Dow Jones tape (or in *The Wall Street Journal,* the next day), you have met SEC disclosure requirements. This does not mean you should neglect other wire services. The story should be given simultaneously to Reuters, Associated Press, and United Press International, and it should be sent by messenger to the business editors of the local newspapers. Only the Dow Jones tape, however, is likely to get the story out immediately to financial news watchers all over the country.

It can be a bit humbling to see your earnings listed alphabetically along with those of dozens of other companies reporting at the same time. One way to spotlight your results is the Dow Jones interview. About 10 days or so before the date on which you plan to release, arrange with the local Dow Jones officer for an exclusive interview in which management provides a general statement about what you expect to report. The statement can be oral, but a written one is better. Although you cannot present final results, you can suggest a range in which per share earnings will fall and also discuss the outlook for the remainder of the year in general terms. Large companies, which have a wide investment following, usually give a Dow Jones interview each quarter. Smaller companies should consider such interviews at midyear and again just before annual sales and earnings are announced. Usually a Dow Jones interview will result in a story, perhaps only a paragraph or two, in a subsequent issue of *The Wall Street Journal.*

When you release financial news, it is wise to have a company financial spokesperson available to answer inquiries from the press. If the information you give and the language you use are clear, the press will seldom ask for more information. When complicated financial situations are involved, however, reporters might ask for clarification, and someone from the company who fully understands the situation should be on hand to give this clarification.

The worst time to release financial news is Friday afternoon. By then, it is usually too late for the Saturday papers to carry the news, and even when it's not, the item might not appear because the Saturday press is notoriously thin in its business news coverage. Sunday papers are not good either, because the special Sunday business section is usually put to bed by Thursday afternoon. With luck, the story will appear on Monday, but it will have to compete with all the other news that piled up over the weekend.

Don't limit making contacts with press people only to when a news story breaks. Building good press relations, like corporate credibility, is a long-term effort. Keep press people informed and interested in your company by sending them at reasonable intervals background information for their files. This works to your advantage in two ways. If the editor does a roundup story on your industry, he may use material at hand, and as a result, your company may get prominent mention in the story. Also, when your press releases reach the editor, it is convenient for him to have a background file in case he wants to round out the story.

In your concern for immediate release, don't overlook the fact that a press release may be of interest to many audiences. It should be mailed to periodicals that cover general business as well as to those devoted to your specific industry. The release can also go to key people on your financial mailing list and, if the news is significant, to shareholders. Receiving a press release, even one that may be several days old, gives many people the feeling of being an insider, which can work to your advantage.

Corporate Publications

The corporate publication is another bulwark of financial communications. Among corporate publications, the annual report is king.

Annual reports tend to follow fads. For a while, it was stunning artwork that made some reports look like high-priced coffee table items. For a brief period, it was simplicity and economy, to impress shareholders with management's concern for their money. You will have to decide whether you wish to follow a fad or start one.

However, certain unchanging facts should be kept in mind regardless of the latest fashion in annual reports.

The annual report should represent the corporation as it wishes to be perceived by shareholders and other investors. Graphics and language create an immediate impression on the reader and should be carefully chosen to make the right impression. The report should contain information that is needed to understand the company—where it is going and why. This information should be presented in readable, interesting form. The report, unless the company has decided to take off in some completely new direction, should follow a basic style each year. Continuity aids credibility.

The letter to shareholders should be a concise, accurate statement. It should tell what happened during the year, how that relates to what transpired in previous years, and how the year's events have affected the company's plans. In essence, each annual report is a chapter in a continuing story, and the shareholders' letter is a summary of the latest chapter. Many, perhaps most, shareholders never get beyond the letter. Even IPs, who are in a hurry, may rely on the letter to decide whether or not they want to know more.

The quarterly, or interim, report shares some of the characteristics of the annual report but on a smaller scale. The publication can be made attractive to readers by reporting major events of the period, perhaps with illustrations for greater interest. Here, too, continuity is desirable. Establish a basic design for the interim and stick to it.

If you don't publish a corporate fact book, perhaps you should. This is a useful tool for the financial community, and it can be sent to shareholders as well. The fact book should look and sound like what it is—a concise reference work containing all the basic information about the company and its industry that an IP would find useful. Graphic excellence is less important here than it is for the annual report, but good organization of the material for easy reference is crucial.

TEAMWORK

As a financial communications manager, you cannot operate in a vacuum. You must have contact with legal and financial people in the company, as well as with top management. Keep in mind that your colleagues are not communicators; they are not supposed to be. At the outset, it will help greatly if they understand your problems as a communicator.

Legal counsel, for example, needs to protect the company by choosing language that does not make the company vulnerable to lawsuits. But legal language may not be understood by most of those who receive corporate communications. Press releases in legalese can be so unintelligible to an editor that he'll toss them into the wastebasket. If he does use them, his readers may be unable to understand the message.

As your first step in solving this problem, make sure you understand what the legal experts are saying and why. Then put the information into language that is as plain as possible without incurring any legal problems. Work with the legal side to refine the language to this point. The same approach should be used with financial and accounting people, whose language may be crystal clear to those in the profession but not to the average reader.

Another problem you will face in assuming the financial communications function is that your deadlines may not be respected or understood by the other members of the team. Financial figures have a way of appearing at the latest possible moment and then are subject to change. Legal counsel may have second thoughts about something already cleared and want to change the language. But you have dates by which, legally, your annual or interim reports must be in the mail. Or you may have to get out a press release immediately to satisfy disclosure requirements or press deadlines.

The sooner your legal and financial colleagues understand your problems, the better. One company arranged a seminar for the legal and accounting departments at which company suppliers who work on the annual report—printers and design people—gave specific examples of the cost of last-minute changes. When they learned how much these changes can mean in terms of overtime and resetting of type, the legal and financial members of the team had a new respect for the communicator's deadlines.

HOW ARE YOU DOING?

Even though the success of a financial communications program cannot be measured on a short-term basis, there are some questions you should ask yourself at regular intervals:

1. Have we promptly reported every significant corporate development to investors as fully as possible?
2. Have we been as diligent in reporting problems and setbacks as we have been in reporting successes?
3. Are our press materials clear, understandable, and useful to editors in the form in which they are released? Are they written in terms the public can grasp?
4. Do corporate publications provide a clear understanding of what the company is doing and why? Is their appearance and tone consistent with how we perceive ourselves as a company?
5. Have we kept in touch with major investment communities during the year through public or private meetings with key investment people?
6. Have our actions followed our words so closely that we have never been challenged to explain an inconsistency?
7. Has our projected performance for any given reporting period been in line with what we actually achieved?
8. Has our financial communications effort, in terms of quality and quantity, been the very best we can produce within the time and money budgeted for this purpose?
9. Do we have a reputation for credibility?

If you answer "yes" to all nine, you have mastered the art of financial communications and are to be congratulated.

9: Community Relations

AN UNDERSTANDING of community relations begins with the premise that the corporation, or organization, is a citizen of the community in which it operates. Such corporate community citizenship involves certain rights and certain responsibilities not unlike those of the individual.

Corporations, like individuals, want a healthy economic climate, good police and fire services, sensible zoning, good schools, and reasonable taxes. In most instances, the interests of the citizens and the business sector are the same. But not always. The business sector sometimes finds itself under fire, particularly in the areas of zoning, taxation, and government regulations. When that happens, the corporation must not only tell its side of the issue but also create an image of itself as a good community citizen.

If you don't begin a community relations program until you're in trouble and need the support of the community, you will probably be too late. Good community relations requires time and constant effort, in good times and bad. Starting a program when it is evident your company wants something from the community can blemish your motives and sincerity for a long time. Clearly, the only successful way to conduct a community relations program is to do it now.

In this chapter, we will raise questions and outline areas of concern for your company in this area and briefly discuss specific tools for handling community relations problems or opportunities. If you need to know more about these tools, we suggest you seek counsel from professionals in the field.[1]

Your first responsibility as a manager in the area of community relations is to understand why your organization needs to be a good community citizen. If you think community relations is just making an occasional charitable donation, then you might ponder these questions:

Are your municipal leaders reacting to the revolt against property taxes by talking about raising business license fees, increasing inventory taxes, or collecting a local payroll tax, with a healthy share contributed by employers?

Are management candidates reluctant to join your company because the local school system has such a poor reputation that they don't want their children attending it?

Do activist groups regard your corporation as a business that takes from the community without contributing anything?

Is crime so common in your area that your employees are afraid to enter or leave the plant during the night?

If a disaster hit your plant or headquarters, could the local emergency services handle the situation?

Are your employees irritated when they get to work because of poor commuting conditions? Does the public transportation system provide good service to your locations?

Would community leaders be sympathetic to your need for a new building, or would they be influenced by no-growth advocates?

If even a few of the above questions seem very familiar to you, then you know how much the community affects your business operation.

While you may not be able to solve the community's problems alone, you can make a contribution of some kind. And if you do, you will be showing community leaders that you are a responsible citizen of the community and willing to work to improve it.

IDENTIFYING THE OPINION LEADERS

In planning a community relations program, you need to know how to reach a varied group of people. The most efficient way is to identify the various subgroups of the community, just as PR programs define their publics. Once the different community groups have been determined, you need to identify the leaders. These generally will be the opinion molders in the community.

Identifying the opinion leaders is not as easy a task as it may seem. Groups of people usually have influence only in certain spheres. For instance, one group may be influential in setting housing policies, while others may be leaders in the area of public transportation. Political figures are not the only community opinion leaders. Educators, top business executives, media people, and presidents of civic organizations are other examples of the types of opinion leaders you will find in most communities.

People in elected or seemingly managerial positions do not always hold the reins of power. In some cities, the elected mayor is the real power broker. In others, it may be an influential publisher or the owner of a major business. Usually, most of the real opinion leaders are known.

If you aren't sure who the real opinion leaders are, your local media people may be a source for this information. Talks with government department heads and officeholders also may give you insight into the situation.

INVOLVING YOUR ORGANIZATION

Involvement in community relations by your organization requires the active, and preferably personal, support of top management. Unless it is apparent that your top management is involved in community relations, the community's opinion leaders may interpret efforts as lip service with no substance.

It is also important to have one person or a department to coordinate the effort. Many large corporations have community affairs or community relations departments within their public relations departments. Some companies assign one person in the PR department to coordinate the effort, with counseling and personnel provided by a public relations firm. Regardless of how the effort is organized, it is important that someone be responsible to make things happen. Community relations is the type of activity that is often ignored in the face of daily crises.

Implementation of a community relations program should not be solely the domain of communications professionals. The resources of various departments should be used, depending on the needs of the program.

One of the ways to involve the various operating units of your company is to establish a community relations policy committee. Such a committee, consisting of various department heads, could meet periodically—perhaps monthly or quarterly—to discuss the needs of the community and to set policy for and monitor the programs. A range of people will give you a varied insight into the needs of the community and make more people available when you need help to carry out a campaign.

If your company has operations in more than one community, don't focus all your efforts on the headquarters city simply because the top brass is there. If you're a large corporation, you may have enough clout in the headquarters city that the efforts there need not be as intensive as efforts in other locations, where your size is not a factor. Often, companies who have their headquarters elsewhere are looked upon as outsiders by city leaders in subsidiary or branch locations.

Community relations in branch locations needs the support and personal attention of local managers, just as your overall effort requires the support and personal attention of corporate management. Although a person from headquarters can provide the tools and guidance for a local community relations effort, the implementation should be by those who actually live and work in the area. A community relations effort that sends mailings or contributions from a headquarters many miles away may only underscore the idea of absentee management.

Many local managers don't realize the inherent value of community relations. They may be more concerned about production quotas, labor problems, and getting next year's budget increased. The first step may be to educate local managers about the value of community relations. The education process will be greatly enhanced if top management makes it clear, either directly or indirectly, that community relations is an important goal of your company. Some organizations make community relations work a mandatory activity of local managers and part of a job performance evaluation.

It is unwise to attempt to present local management with a prepackaged program. Instead, let the local people define the needs of their communities and work with them in developing a program for their situation. A person who has had a voice in developing a project will be more eager to participate in it than in a project that was merely assigned to him.

Community Relations Starts at Home

A community's perception of a company derives principally from the company's employees. Employees are ambassadors, good or bad, to the community. Their views and feelings about their company are transmitted to the community as a whole. Good community relations starts at home. Obviously, if you have employees who are unhappy and bad-mouth the company, then any community relations effort will be an uphill battle.

If you have limited resources and have to choose between a community relations program and an employee relations program, you're probably better off emphasizing employee relations. At least you'll be getting some benefit in terms of community relations as a result of more contented and better informed employees. Ideally, you should be making a major effort among both of these important publics—the community and your employees.

Employee and community relations can be combined to some extent by having employees at all levels participate in your community relations activities. Often the most valuable contribution a company can make to the community is the time and talents of its employees. Such involvement can create an effective program and boost employee morale. Many employees have jobs that offer little in the way of recognition or satisfaction. Often these employees can get a real feeling of accomplishment and service by participating in a community relations program. It's hard to take pride in putting the same wheel assembly on a car every day when you don't get to see the satisfied customer. But planning and building a youth baseball field brings much-needed satisfaction to a worker at the opening day ceremony.

If you decide to involve your employees in a community relations project, make sure it is done on a strictly voluntary basis. You probably won't have any trouble finding enough employees for your activities on such a basis. Don't antagonize those who don't want to participate by using pressure tactics on them.

Chief Executive Leadership Is Important

Your community relations effort will lack impact if it does not have the involvement of the chief executive officer. A 1978 survey of the Fortune 1000 companies revealed that chief executive officers devoted about 40 percent of their personal time to public issues. This was twice as much as just two years earlier.[2]

These executives would not spend that amount of time on public issues unless they were sure it is of vital interest to their businesses. Although your chief executive may not need to spend 40 percent of his time on public issues—which admittedly includes more than what is generally considered community relations—it is important for him to be personally and visibly involved.

In formulating your community relations program, remember that as a citizen of the community your organization has a right, and a responsibility, to speak out on issues, whether or not they affect your company directly. Depending on the personality of your chief executive, you may want to arrange forums or speaking platforms for him to speak out on important issues that affect your community. National issues often have an impact on local communities. The media often seek local experts to comment on national stories. For example, Congress may pass legislation to stimulate employment through an employer tax incentive program. Your chief executive's opinion of the impact of the program on your community would be newsworthy.

The Larger Picture

Community relations also encompasses the corporation's responsiveness in serving the changing needs of society. This total approach has come to be known as corporate social responsibility.

Corporate social responsibility is based on the belief that business has more than the traditional responsibility of making a profit and thereby providing employment and contributing to the economic well-being of society. Business, according to this premise, also has the responsibility to help society with those profits. Many large corporations, operating in fields that are under attack by various pressure groups, have cataloged the activities they have undertaken to achieve corporate responsibility.

One such company is the Standard Oil Company of California. In the preface to his company's booklet on corporate citizenship, John R. Grey, president, states that his company is aware that its long-term success depends on its responsiveness to society's evolving needs and to the creation of a climate in which the business can grow and flourish.

> As a corporate citizen, we have a strong interest in the quality of life in the communities in which we have operations and business interests. In them, we strive to help provide quality educational, medical, cultural and recreational activities. Healthy communities attract employees of high caliber, as well as other responsible citizens, such as suppliers and customers, upon whom the company depends.[3]

The booklet contains sections on the company's activities in such areas as equal opportunity and affirmative action employment programs; preserving, protecting, and beautifying the environment; product testing and customer service operation; local community projects; and education and support of the arts.

As you can see by this example, corporate social responsibility includes more than just traditional community relations activities. It really reflects the philosophy of the company.

Even if you don't have a structured community relations program, you probably have a number of activities that fall within the area of corporate social responsibility. We suggest that you compile a list of all your activities that fall under this general heading. Such a list will enable you and the company's top management to evaluate what your company is doing in this area. Having a clear picture of your company's programs will arm you against any criticism that might arise.

Cataloging your efforts also allows you to review them periodically in the context of a total corporate responsibility effort. As Standard Oil concluded in summarizing its past achievements: "As a corporate citizen in an era when many institutions are under scrutiny, we are constantly updating our goals and the standards against which we appraise our conduct."

A "RADICAL-LIBERAL" EXAMPLE

Tom Harris, Levi Strauss & Company's community affairs director, calls Levi's program the "rad-lib" of community relations efforts. He's not talking about the politics of the effort but rather about Levi's unusually strong, long-standing commitment to community relations.

The program is so comprehensive that a book on the company's history, *Levi's* by Ed Cray,[4] contains a chapter on the community relations effort. The chapter's title, "Far Too Little Competition," indicates the uniqueness of Levi's efforts. That a history of the company would contain an entire chapter on community relations in itself says something about Levi's dedication to the effort. Indeed, there may well be too little competition in the area. Undoubtedly, many companies' community relations efforts would rate little more than a footnote in a chronicle of their history.

As Levi's readily admits, its community relations efforts won't necessarily work for everyone. Levi's case history is presented here because of the totality of its admirable program. It also contains examples of some self-admitted mistakes that can be avoided.

Perhaps the most radical element of Levi's community affairs program is the specific and well-defined policy and set of guidelines the company has for the entire operation. This doesn't mean the program isn't flexible, but rather the activities always fit into one of four well-thought-out areas of concern: health, education, human resources, and community and cultural development. How Levi's participates in those areas of concern generally falls into three types of activities: special programs; national, regional, and capital contributions; and direct service grants to community programs in the Southwest and Southeast, where most of the company's plants are located.

Of these activities, the special programs are the most innovative. During the late 1970s, Levi's developed special programs that deal with specific nationwide problems but are implemented in local communities. The plan is to initiate local activities that will, in time, become self-sustaining. No project is undertaken that will collapse as soon as Levi's withdraws its participation. Levi's enters these projects with the assumption that after a few years the company will no longer be involved in their funding. As a result, funds can be allocated to programs in other areas of the country as soon as earlier programs become self-supporting. This fits another goal of the special programs projects: to develop a network of similar programs across the country.

Levi's is currently sponsoring special programs that address themselves to a variety of social issues, including the needs of the aging, the battered family, the quality of management in nonprofit agencies, community education, small town and rural programming, and corporate social responsibility. Efforts in the corporate social responsibility area are designed to stimulate other corporations to take a more active role. Levi's seeks to promote an understanding of the ways that corporations can be encouraged to become more active in social involvement. One of the company's means of reaching this objective is by awarding grants to graduate schools of business to develop curriculums dealing with the topic of corporate social responsibility.

Typically, Levi's special programs consist of grants for research or training of professionals to deal with these problems on a local level. For instance, the special program directed at the needs of the aging has included grants for a demonstration program for a campus-based community training center in gerontological services, a training seminar for professionals who provide services for senior citizens, and a seminar for the Gray Panthers to help them strengthen their administrative services.

In addition to awarding its own grants, Levi's also seeks funding for its special programs from private foundations, other corporations, and government agencies. This is in keeping with the policy of not having a program depend solely on Levi's for support but rather of having it become self-sustaining through other means of funding.[5]

An important element of Levi's community affairs program is the participation of local employees in "community involvement teams." Although the participation of rank-and-file employees is voluntary, local managers know that community involvement is an important part of their job function. Not only are their job evaluations based in part on the success of their community involvement teams, but management bonuses are often paid for outstanding performance in this area. Community involvement teams, which have been operating for more than 10 years now, exist in 60 domestic facilities. Teams can select their own projects, but they are encouraged to participate in efforts that are within the company's overall community affairs goals. Often teams engage in fund-raising activities—such as bake sales, auctions, or contests—to help an organization of their choice. Other activities include collecting food from employees for senior citizens, sponsoring blood drives, and donating the services of employees to local organizations. Employee-volunteers have painted Girl Scout clubhouses, taken orphans to baseball games, and arranged Easter egg hunts for retarded children.

Levi's does not expect to succeed in all areas of concern and divisions of operation. It specifically allocates 5 percent of its community relations funds to high-risk efforts. The company believes it is important not only to fund traditional programs but to take a chance on innovative answers to society's problems.

Part of Levi's current policy has evolved as a result of past mistakes. When Levi's first started a structured community affairs department in 1968, it was a time of transition for the company's charitable efforts. Levi's had previously allocated almost all of its community relations funds to conventional cultural and educational philanthropies in its headquarters city, San Francisco. After a study by an employee policy committee, the emphasis was shifted from headquarters to the communities. It was also decided to enter the area of social problems rather than just support the arts and higher education.

The first efforts in this direction were not successful. In an attempt to support minority retail clothing stores, Levi's acted too paternalistically toward the small businesses. A crash course in retailing for the businesses proved to be insufficient. Worse yet, the fledgling companies were given false economic support. Levi's allowed the companies a year to pay bills and provided professional services such as accounting and legal assistance on a volunteer basis. When Levi's generous credit expired, it found the minority companies were not used to prompt payment of bills. Levi's learned that if you're going to help someone you can't forget your business sense.

Because the results are hard to measure, community relations is a difficult concept to sell in these days of cause and effect relationships in almost every segment of the production and marketing process. Community relations, we believe, is worth the effort. The importance of doing good work in the community and making these activities known will pay off and help make substantial contributions to the company's overall corporate goals.

REFERENCES

1. Scott Cutlip and Allen Center, *Effective Public Relations* (Englewood Cliffs, N.J.: Prentice-Hall, 1971). Chapter 14, "The Community Public," is an excellent source of how-to information.
2. Robert L. Fegley, "New Breed Top Executive Takes Charge," *Los Angeles Times* (December 31, 1978).
3. *Working Toward a Better Society* (San Francisco: Standard Oil Company of California, 1977).
4. Ed Cray, *Levi's* (Princeton: N.J.: Houghton Mifflin, 1978).
5. For further information on Levi's special programs, see *Special Programs* (San Francisco: Levi Strauss & Company, 1978), available from Levi Strauss Foundation, Two Embarcadero Center, San Francisco, California 94106.

10: Labor-Management Communications

THE CHARACTER of the American worker is changing. Although the traditional pattern remains the same—the old retire and the young go to work—the attitudes and aspirations of the young are far different from those held by the older employees when they first started. The ideas and attitudes of these newer employees will have a significant influence on the businesses and industries for which they work. Management will have a good deal to say about how the workers are motivated and rewarded. And the ability of management to stimulate these employees to be productive will largely determine corporate performance.

But the change in people and attitudes is creating a new set of problems for management. In this chapter, we will point out some potential problem areas. And we will suggest ways that will help you understand and communicate with your new and old employees. But first, we must determine who these new employees are and what makes them different.

THE CHANGING WORKFORCE

We should not think of the new employees as being "out there" someplace. They are our sons and daughters.

In our employee attitude work at Ketchum MacLeod & Grove, we often hear managers criticize younger employees for lacking the traditional work ethic. Yet surveys by our agency and other firms show the desire to do a good job is deeply rooted in these workers. The change is not in the desire but in the motivation. Younger workers value self-fulfillment as well as material success. This can mean that if psychological rewards are not offered, employee performance can suffer. Employees are becoming less loyal to their companies but more dedicated to their occupational disciplines or professions.

Management must contend with the rising expectations of employees—expectations that may not always be easily fulfilled. The growing tendency of young workers is to believe that they are entitled as a matter of social right to a meaningful job and all its benefits, including secure retirement and health care coverage. These expectations are part of what one researcher calls the "spreading psychology of entitlement."

When expectations are not met, employees can become highly vocal—even militant—about their discontent. As part of their education, employees are being taught to question and examine. This can lead to conflicts with management on day-to-day operations. Answers based on authority alone ("We do it this way because I say so") will not be effective in the long run.

The changing profile of the American worker is being affected by the increase of working women. More American women are working today than ever before. In 1960, women comprised only 33 percent of the national labor force. By 1978, the percentage had risen to approximately 41 percent. Among reasons cited by economists are: (1) widespread communications that have helped to create a higher standard of living, so that a husband's income is often not enough to meet his family's perceived needs; (2) a growing number of women who have substituted careers for religion as an outlet for their energies and skills; and (3) the rise in the number of divorces in the United States, which has reached one million a year, making marriage less stable financially than it used to be.

The earnings of the working wife sometimes place the family in a relatively affluent class. Obvious financial rewards, higher education, supportive government actions, and a general rise in the age at which women marry and bear children are all factors in the phenomenon. The result is increasing affluence among employees through untraditional means.

This, then, is the picture of the type of employee who will shortly come to dominate the American labor scene: a better educated, more affluent person with higher expectations than ever before, a desire for self-fulfillment through good performance, and greater loyalty to what he does rather than whom he does it for. Many of the people who will fill entry-level management positions will come directly from the college campus. At one time, top management took pride in filling these positions through internal promotions, often from the ranks of hourly employees, supplemented by hiring from outside the company. It was a delicate balance. Now the balance has been upset by the pressure of competition, technology, and management's increasing complexity. Unfortunately, this has closed a channel of upward mobility for production workers, a frustrating development for many of them. The widening gap between worker and supervisor could lead to absenteeism, apathy, work disruptions, and lower morale and productivity.

On the other hand, it is troublesome to discover that a large number of middle and supervisory managers find their work only minimally satisfying at best, according to a study by a national association. White collar dissatisfaction can have many causes, such as too much interference from supervisors, an inability to participate in decisionmaking, or too little opportunity to pursue interesting ideas.

Basic issues, such as wages and hours, can also be part of the problem. Although nearly a quarter of all professional and managerial employees regularly work overtime, only a small percentage are paid for the extra effort. Top management often sees nothing wrong with this. They allow lower-echelon white collar employees to be discontent. A job title may be the only reward.

This can lead to white collar unionization. Labor unions have been making significant gains among white collar workers in recent years. White collar employees with close ties to organized production workers are often prime targets because alert shop stewards can sense any widespread unhappiness and pass the information along to union leaders.

Of the 100 million persons employed in the United States, approximately 75 percent are not members of a union. This figure is likely to decline in the years ahead. Although unions currently are having trouble in their organizing efforts, this is not by any means a permanent condition. Management should not be lulled into a false sense of security. Younger and far more aggressive labor leaders are already talking of new organizing drives, new methods of enhancing labor's political push. That means management will be faced with a more expensive way of doing business, because unions are expensive.

Surveys have shown that the employment costs of unionized companies are higher than those of nonunion companies—as much as 25 percent higher. This is not because union employees make substantially more than nonunion employees but because of redundant employees, narrow job description, restricted production, strikes, and slowdowns. These result in lower productivity and many companies find it difficult to compete for sales, particularly in the world market.

The attitudes of the new employee, whether unionized or not, will undoubtedly cause some problems in the years ahead. In the article entitled "Futurologist's Overview: The American Workplace of the 1980s," in the September 1978 issue of *Occupational Hazards,* Peter J. Sheridan noted that relations between management and labor "will be under considerable stress in the next 10 to 15 years. Women and minorities will be demanding their rights in the workplace. OSHA regulations . . . will be debated vigorously, as will a national pension policy. These and other factors could upset the equilibrium of management–labor relationships."

While there are no magic solutions to the problems management will face in the years ahead, employer–employee relations are the key to arriving at some solutions—and crucial to these relations is communication.

Communication can no longer be considered a choice of management. Rather, it is the essence of management. Communication determines what happens in our companies. Frequently, the quality of management's communications effort determines the final quality of the effort our employees make.

IMPROVING COMMUNICATIONS IN THE NONUNIONIZED COMPANY

Companies must examine how they can improve communications with today's employee, so they can communicate effectively with tomorrow's employee. We believe that employees today often want to tell management how they feel, but too many companies don't know how to listen. Management frequently lacks the time, the patience, the channels, or the objectivity to really listen to the employees.

Those managers who do listen are sometimes not aware of the different factors that can distort the communications process. For example, employees must have the confidence that management will not take advantage of them if they speak their mind. If managers become upset by what employees tell them, then employees are likely to refrain from speaking up. An employee who believes that disclosure of his or her feelings might lead management to block the attainment of a personal goal may deliberately conceal or distort those feelings.

Another problem is one that is often referred to as the "cascade effect." The principle is the same as that in a game of "Gossip," in which a message is whispered from one person to the next, down a long line. Inevitably, there is a wide discrepancy between the original message and what the last individual hears. The same thing happens in business communications, either from top management cascading down or up from various employee levels up to higher management.

Communications-oriented managers supply employees with meaningful information on the company's goals, sales, production achievements, and financial health. When making changes in employee policy or in plant equipment or tooling, they notify the workforce in advance and explain the changes. They use persuasion, rather than pressure, to obtain desired productivity. By monitoring employee attitudes, they become aware of what employees are saying or not saying and what makes them respond and what turns them off. Such managers realize that what is effective with one employee group may not work with another. In sum, they establish sound two-way communications.

Establishing a Grievance Procedure

An effective grievance procedure helps keep employees receptive to company communications. Employees should have a way to discuss their problems, real or imagined, and find solutions. If not, they will believe little of what the company tells them thereafter on any matter. They can become prime targets for the union organizer who promises them solutions to their problems. They believe the organizer because they want to. Furthermore, if the union wins the election, it can deliver, because a grievance procedure is the major advantage that a union offers. Virtually all union contracts call for grievance procedures. It is disconcerting to learn, however, that only a small percentage of all nonunionized employers have some means by which their employees can register complaints.

Grievance procedures in most nonunionized companies tend to operate with mixed results. In some cases, management will initiate the procedure and then fail to monitor it through employee attitude surveys or interviews. In other cases, first-line supervisors, some of whom have no training in human relations, will suppress problems, fearing that complaints about their activities will reflect poorly on them if those complaints reach higher management. This, of course, defeats the very purpose of the grievance procedure.

Despite these potential difficulties, grievance procedures in nonunionized firms can and do work effectively. Where they do work, they all have one thing in common—they get at the root of problems and seek solutions. Where they seek merely to passify the employee or to give the individual " an opportunity to get it off his chest," they make no genuine effort to find a solution. The problems do not disappear; they only resurface in new ways.

Most grievance procedures are structured in a similar manner.

The employee can take the complaint to his or her immediate supervisor. If that action fails to result in a satisfactory solution, the employee may take the complaint to a company-appointed employee relations representative or put the complaint in writing and send it to the personnel department. Usually, some satisfactory solution is reached. In rare cases where a grievance remains unsolved after it has gone to personnel, it can be taken to a top management officer in the company, whose decision is final.

We are not attempting to present step-by-step rules for initiating grievance procedures but only to point out the benefits of having such a system. The procedure provides an outlet for employee frustrations. It allows upward communication from employees to higher levels of management. It encourages a dialogue with management rather than with union organizers or sympathizers. It helps keep employees receptive to company communications and enhances the credibility of such communications.

Once a grievance procedure has been established, it should be communicated to employees through regular channels, such as a brochure, the company house organ, and group meetings with employees and their supervisors. Managers should remember that the purpose of establishing a grievance procedure is not to win disputes with employees but to foster goodwill, to let your employees know that you care about their problems and are willing to help solve them. Employees will respond favorably to this positive foundation.

Attitude Surveys: The Ability to Listen

Before effective communications can take place, managers must know how to listen. They must monitor employee attitudes. This is of critical importance because attitudes influence on-the-job behavior—productivity, initiative, work quality, and wage and benefits demands. Employee attitude surveys can serve as an early warning system. If the nonunionized company neglects to monitor employee attitudes, you can be sure that the professional union organizer won't neglect it.

The union organizer makes it his business to know what the

workers are thinking and to capitalize on those attitudes that are likely to lead to unionization. Similarly, company managers should know what their employees are thinking, too. This enables them to spot festering problems and make corrections before those problems surface as anticompany action.

There are many kinds of attitude surveys and many public opinion researchers. A technique used by Ketchum MacLeod & Grove to survey attitudes and opinions has proved to be very effective. Our goal in developing an attitudes survey is to determine the feelings of workers toward communications in a given company. This isn't restricted to the company's house organ and its other formal communications media. It includes all means of conveying messages from one person to another, verbally as well as by memos and letters.

Such a survey tells us more about other conditions existing in the total employment atmosphere than about communications per se.

This is accomplished through the structure and methods of the interviews. Our interviewers are all trained not only in opinion and attitude survey techniques but also as journalists, with experience in interviewing people in many different situations. A typical survey proceeds as follows. First, we draw a statistical sampling of the people to be interviewed. Their identities are not revealed, and the statements given in the report are not attributed to anyone. Anonymity is important in obtaining the employees' cooperation and confidence.

Employees are selected for interviews in two ways. When dealing with nonprofessional employees, a sampling of supervisors is interviewed. Foremen and other supervisory personnel reflect a valid sampling of the opinions of large numbers of blue collar employees who work with them, and such a sample avoids the possibility of complaints from employee unions, if they exist. In surveys of professional employees, those at the lowest level are interviewed, because they are larger in number and there is no chance of union complaint.

Our specialists conduct the interviews in a number of predetermined locations, usually closed rooms. No tape recorders or other mechanical recording devices are used. Workers are informed within the preceding 48 hours that they will be included in the survey.

Before the employees' arrival, the interviewer carefully reviews a specific list of objectives that guide him in structuring the discussion. Although he does, to some extent, attempt to guide the interview's direction, he asks few specific questions. By handling the interview in this way, the opinion researcher gradually uncovers the matters that really interest and concern the employee.

The discussion may take a turn such as this:

Researcher: What do you think about the photos in the company house organ?

Employee: Fine, but I see too many shots of those guys in the XYZ department. I don't know what they did to deserve so much publicity. They never pay any attention to the suggestions the fellows in my section make. And talk about communication—they never tell us anything!

This is not an extreme example. Statements of this kind turn up many times during a set of interviews.

The interviews are usually terminated after about 45 minutes. When the employee leaves, the researcher rapidly records his impressions of the employee's opinions as accurately as possible.

After all the interviews are completed, the comments are categorized, and an overall report is prepared. The report usually begins with a section on general impressions developed in the total survey. These are amplified in interpretive sections based on individual impressions. At the end of the report, an appendix categorizes all the comments for further analysis by the client.

Our surveys have uncovered a number of specific problems. Sometimes these problems come as a surprise to management.

For example, while interviewing employees of a large meat packing company, we found employee relations problems varied from plant to plant. One plant had severe communications problems because many of the employees were recent immigrants from Poland who did not understand English. Interviews in this facility also reflected problems that were common to the entire organization. There were feelings that management had no overall plan for company development, that advancement opportunities were extremely limited, that employees were generally overworked, that top management ignored the individual worker, that he had no place to take his grievances, and that management really didn't care about his problems. The frequency of these complaints suggested that a carefully programmed and broad-scale alteration of company policies would be needed to correct, or eliminate, most areas of company-wide discontent.

In another case, we conducted interviews in two divisions of a large engineering and manufacturing firm. Although we were primarily concerned with the state of communications in this company, we also were alert for employee attitudes relating to a possible strike that was anticipated when the existing contract ran out. We found a sensitivity to the favorable settlements labor had won in similar companies, evidence of disenchantment with an incentive pay system that was in effect, and general dissatisfaction with the pension plan. All these factors were moving the hourly employees toward a strike, especially the young employees concentrated in one division where we conducted interviews. On the basis of our findings, we predicted a walkout.

In general, we found that wages would probably be the big issue in the upcoming contract negotiations. Our evaluation also suggested pension, incentive pay, grievances, and layoffs would be significant issues. As we predicted, these were the significant issues when the strike occurred as we had predicted.

A bakery company where we conducted an attitude survey presented a different picture. Here, we talked to employees of a company that had poor profits. Management and many employees anticipated a rosier future. In the course of the survey, we found the middle managers were frequently dubious of top management's intentions, and there was a tendency in older employees to regret the end of paternalism that once was characteristic of company officials. We discovered that hourly employees were surprisingly content. But we also found a lagging company loyalty, a concern over lack of recognition by management, and a rather cavalier attitude concerning product quality.

A survey of employees of an industrial toolmaking company revealed the primary sources of employee discontent were job security, a suspicion that management was unfriendly, subcontracting of work, and an antagonistic union.

We don't believe that all companies are afflicted with these problems. But, with the increase in mechanization, the growing prevalence of the psychology of entitlement, and the rising expectations of the new employee we discussed earlier, we are going to face more employee dissatisfaction.

Management can at least attenuate problems before they reach a dangerous stage. But management must know that the problems exist. Many companies are not aware of the discontent breeding among their employees. The only way they can uncover such problems is to use an external objective source to assess employee attitudes.

Certainly, surveys of employee attitudes cannot replace the paternalistic boss–worker relationship that existed in many shops. But surveys can help to improve communications and modify working conditions so that workers, both salaried and nonsalaried, will be more satisfied. There are also financial benefits for the employer who is aware of the emotional needs of his people: Production levels will be maintained and increased by a force of happy employees, the possibilities of unionization will be reduced, and potential difficulties with the federal government on the status of minority employees may be prevented.

Dealing with the Union Organizing Campaign

Experience shows that if management attempts to communicate with employees only after a union organizing drive has started, such communication will have little credibility. Regular communications, downward and upward, well in advance of the union organizing attempt are the most productive.

When a union election date is set, both the union and the company escalate their communications efforts. Surveys have shown that the most effective means involve oral communications. In the case of the company, the most influential effort has been group meetings at which employees are addressed by top company executives. Next in effectiveness are individual talks by supervisors, followed by home mailings.

An example of combining these techniques for the best results is found in two back-to-back campaigns by a company with a record of sound employee relations policies, continuing employee communications, and periodic attitude surveys. These practices are obviously the result of enlightened management.

The company had been the target of numerous union organizing attempts over the years, but this was the first time it faced an organizing campaign by a powerful major union. The company wasn't about to be lulled into a false sense of security because of its past record of winning in union organizing attempts. Company management gave the election top priority and prepared for the toughest fight it ever faced.

The entire campaign required one month of intensive effort. The target of the first drive was more than 900 production and maintenance employees. To the union, they represented about $100,000 a year in dues.

A communications program was implemented throughout a four-week period. The program was intensive, using all types of public relations tools, including letters to the employees at their homes, slide presentations with follow-up brochures, posters in the plant, and very importantly, talks by the board chairman to employee groups. Emphasis was placed on the union's strike record and a comparison of the company's benefits with those of unionized plants in the area.

The union conducted a campaign that was equally intensive. Union organizers distributed as much literature and spoke to employees just as often as management did.

The election turned into a cliff-hanger, but the company won in a close vote. Although the election had been won, the company's employee communications efforts didn't end. Slide presentations and brochures were prepared to inform the employees of their benefits. The union, having lost by such a small margin, filed for an election the following year. Again, the company responded with literature, slide presentations, posters, speeches, and a series of letters. The campaign by the union was even more intense than in the first election, resorting to distortions and personal attacks. The company countered with facts to disprove misinformation. This time, the company won the election by a two-to-one margin.

In both of these campaigns, the company effectively used the three techniques we noted earlier—group meetings by top management, individual talks and presentations by supervisors, and home mailings along with other distribution of literature. The effectiveness of such communications techniques was enhanced by the company's record of sound employee policies and consistent employee communications all year round. Within that framework, communications can play a vital role in election campaigns.

Other efforts in an election campaign include films, newsletters, payroll stuffers, charts, handout literature, house organ articles, and employee picnics and dinners. Such tools, however, should be used to support, not substitute for, personal communications by top management and supervisors.

Legal Guidelines in Campaign Communications

An executive who is responsible for communications in a union election will need legal counsel. All written communications to employees during an organizing drive should be reviewed in advance by a labor attorney to avoid the possibility of an unfair labor practice. The rule of thumb for the nonlegal executive is this: Put nothing in writing about the union unless it can be accurately documented.

The acronym TIPS may be applied to all written and oral communications: Never *T*hreaten, never *I*nterrogate, never *P*romise, and never engage in Surveillance of employees. In addition, be careful how often you focus on strikes in communcations. Too much emphasis on strikes could be construed as a veiled threat that a strike is inevitable if the union wins because the company would not bargain in good faith, and the union might file for an unfair labor practice ruling by the National Labor Relations Board.

Foremen and other supervisors should understand the importance of their role in shaping employee attitudes. The supervisor is the key. What he says and does may ultimately determine the success or failure of the union's campaign. Remember, whatever a supervisor says to employees during a campaign can be binding. Such statements can be held against the company just as though a top company official had made them. Unless supervisors have had experience in dealing with organizing attempts, management should provide a training course to inform them of what they can and cannot do and say, to avoid charges of unfair labor practice.

The common ground rules of no threats, interrogation, promises, and surveillance apply, of course, to the supervisor. Ketchum MacLeod & Grove has compiled a list used in supervisor training sessions that explains the dos and don'ts in election campaigns.

CHALLENGE FOR THE FUTURE

The day is long past when employers could dictate employee policies and practices without much regard for their acceptance. Today's employees, unlike the generation that preceded them, have a great tendency to question, to examine, and to rebel against anything they do not understand or do not perceive to be in their best interest. The next generation of employees may go further still—possibly outside the company to courts, environmental groups, consumer activists, and government agencies.

Most employees undoubtedly first will go through company channels to have problems solved. To accommodate this the company's environment for free speech, for effective two-way communications, must be preserved and nurtured. This will be one of the major corporate challenges of the future.

Inherent in every challenge is the opportunity to meet it success-fully. We offer six points that management should adopt in communicating with both the union and nonunion employee:

1. Management must become more responsive to human values when relating to employees. Communications must address their needs for understanding, for dignity, and, ultimately, for hope.

2. Employee communications, as any other corporate function, must be planned and must be operative throughout the year to achieve continuity and credibility.

3. A company's grievance procedure must enable employees to receive direct and empathetic hearings that result in equitable solutions.

4. Front-line supervisors must remain responsive to employee needs, fully recognizing that, to the employee, the supervisor is the company.

5. In spite of the increasing complexity of the corporate structure, top management must not lose touch with the rank and file. Management must develop the ability to listen to employees as well as to talk to them.

6. Management must pay considerable attention to the direction, quality and content of all communications with employees.

Labor–management communications, based on these guidelines, is not the solution to all of management's problems. It can, however, make a significant contribution to building mutual understanding, trust, and cooperation—the key to sound labor–management relations.

11: Executive Communications

THE EFFECTIVENESS of a company's executives as spokespeople can often make the difference between success and failure in the execution of many public relations projects. All of the efforts of the public relations director in preparing for a key event can be wasted if the chief executive officer is inadequate in that role. Conversely, an effective corporate spokesperson can strongly complement any public relations effort. Credibility is determined not only by what you say, but also by how you say it. In this chapter we will examine how the public relations director can help to improve the communications skills of management.

In developing a program to improve the effectiveness of executive communications efforts, the public relations director must first examine the environment in which those activities take place. Several factors need to be considered. First, the public's confidence in business has slipped in the past 10 years. Second, the operations of the business community, especially of the larger corporations, are becoming increasingly complex. And third, the news media, through which the executive must communicate much of the time, are generally skeptical and uninformed in the operations of the business community.

PUBLIC CONFIDENCE

A recent public opinion survey clearly showed the public's declining confidence in American business. Only 20 percent of the public indicated confidence in the business community, and only 8 percent gave it "high approval." Ten years earlier, the same survey had indicated that 55 percent of the public expressed confidence in business. An important reason for this decline in confidence is the well-documented reluctance of many business executives to speak out on the issues facing their companies. In another poll, less than 3 percent of the public could identify the heads of our largest corporations, including General Motors, AT&T, Gulf Oil, and Ford Motor Company. Yet in that same poll consumer activists were widely recognized. More than three-fourths of the public could identify Ralph Nader, Gloria Steinem, and public figures. These people are well known because they are media personalities—they communicate their points of view, opinions, opposition, or support to the American public. They face the TV cameras and the newspaper reporters frequently.

The business community must recognize that there are gigantic public debates going on, and it is barely participating. Corporate executives, through their reluctance to speak out on issues affecting their businesses, are inadvertently creating an extremely negative public climate in which their business must operate.

A negative public climate affects business in three critical ways: First, the legitimacy of business is slowly eroded, leading to calls by the public for government regulation. That regulation costs American business a fortune. It complicates the operating environment, and makes it difficult for any business to compete. Second, a poor image causes antagonism and a loss of bargaining power at the negotiating table. Labor problems continue to grow, even as business offers higher and higher wages and benefits. Finally, a tarnished image discourages the best and brightest young people from entering the field. In fact, today business receives one of the lowest ratings among those fields covered by surveys conducted on-campus.

The answer to this plight is quite clear. The business executives of today must begin to employ the same strategies and zeal in selling their points of views that they use in selling their products. By planning a communications strategy and by helping key executives use the media constructively, the public relations director can begin to win favor for his company's efforts in the press and, through the press, with the public.

There are several ways that the public relations director can help executives present their points of view:

1. *Start with a thorough personal knowledge of the company's operations.* There is no excuse for a PR director who does not know why the company's ratios have been declining for the past nine months.

2. *Know the rules.* A thorough study of Securities and Exchange Commission (SEC) and New York Stock Exchange regulations on disclosures of financial information, for example, is critical. You'll inevitably find yourself in a room some day when the auditor says "You can't say that." A good PR director must know what the rules *will* let executives say.

3. *Be sensitive to the audience.* Help your executives learn to adapt their presentations of financial data to the needs of the audience. Be the representative of that audience with your executives and give your opinion of the audience needs and wants. An in-depth explanation of an item like "earnings before extraordinary item" might be critical in an interview with an analyst from Morgan Stanley, for example, but largely irrelevant to a reporter from an industry trade publication.

4. *Play the devil's advocate.* Anticipate the questions of your audience about the financial statements and help your executives prepare direct, concise responses to those questions.

5. *Suggest training when it is needed.* Recommending training to an executive who needs it is a job for the PR director. It's not an easy job, but everyone will be a lot better off after it's done. (The kinds of training available is discussed in detail later in this chapter.)

With this type of help from the PR director, the executive will be best able to represent the company by taking on the role of spokesperson.

A SKEPTICAL PRESS

Executives must be prepared to work with the media. For some reason, many businesspeople assume that reporters know as much as or more than they themselves know. Of course, the reverse is true. A reporter can never know as much about a company as the executive knows. Few reporters have a business education. Practically none have personal managerial experience.

In addition, a great many reporters enter an interview situation skeptical of the integrity of the company, of the integrity of the executive, and of the legitimacy of the story. It is critical that the public relations director thoroughly prepare the executive for each interview by covering the following topics.

1. *The publication.* What has it published about the company or the industry recently? What is its general tone? What kind of story is likely to appeal to the editors?
2. *The reporter.* Is the person conducting the interview a veteran or a novice? What is his or her degree in? What kind of attitude toward the company does the reporter bring to the interview?
3. *The story.* Be sure your executive is thoroughly prepared, and be sure you know the story well yourself. During the interview, be prepared to suggest to the executive points that might otherwise go unmentioned.

Brief the executive the day before an interview. Include what you've learned about the publication and the reporter, and prepare a written summary of the key points to be covered. In the case of a broadcast interview, be sure to clearly define your company's objective, and use the techniques outlined later in this chapter to keep that objective in the forefront of your executive's mind.

THE EXECUTIVE'S ROLE IN CORPORATE COMMUNICATIONS

There was a time in the history of business when the senior executives were the only spokespeople any company had. But in today's corporate framework, many members of middle management find themselves, to one degree or another, involved as spokespeople for the company. In many cases, this is a result of the complex operations of giant companies. The president of West-inghouse Electric Corporation could not possibly answer the inquiries of his thousands of stockholders, let alone the press, the financial community, and the public.

But the executive who uses the logistics as an excuse for inaccessibility may be shirking his responsibility and missing an opportunity to have his company's story told. There are at least three ways the executive can participate in the communications activities of his company to fulfill that responsibility and to take advantage of that opportunity.

1. As one who speaks for the corporation in the business and financial community, with the government, and to the press.
2. As a news source both on the affairs of his company and on the activities in the world that affect the company.
3. As a communicator with the community—an active contributor to the environment in which his company operates.

The Executive as a Business Spokesperson

Personal contact with the key groups should be the leading edge of any executive communications effort. Everyone, from legislator to odd-lot stockholder, likes to say, "Just the other day I heard the president of the company say. . . ." There are some times when only the chief executive officer will do as a spokesperson. Most CEOs do make appearances at annual stockholders' meetings and at security analysts societies, and engage in occasional interviews with reporters from *The Wall Street Journal* or from local papers.

Executives are welcome participants in business forums, where they can share their perspective on economic or industry trends. They can and should present the perspective of their companies to business and industry groups. Government bodies are constantly inviting public comment on issues that are critically important to business and on which business executives can speak with authority. By addressing local and federal legislative bodies, executives have the opportunity to (1) ensure that their company's perspective is considered, (2) demonstrate that the company is taking the matter seriously, and (3) give the CEO valuable experience at fielding questions from outsiders.

The financial community puts a great premium on direct contact with senior management. In addition to attending the large, broad-based meetings of analysts societies, CEOs should consider meeting with individual groups of large investors, financial institutions, or stockbrokers. Regional or annual meetings are good opportunities for those appearances.

The Executive as a News Source

Through regular meetings with local and national print and broadcast media, executives can achieve a great deal of recognition for themselves and their companies. By working to educate the press, through regular contact, the executive can also ensure a more well-formed reception for the company's ongoing communications effort in key media.

CEOs should meet regularly with editors from business and financial publications, newspapers, radio and television, and perhaps even key trade publications in their industries. Subjects for discussion can include external factors affecting the company, its employees, or stockholders; internal aspects of the company's progress, or lack of it; progress of capital spending programs; R&D breakthroughs; and so forth. In addition to these regular meetings, CEOs should meet with local newspaper editors in key cities around the country. In those cities and towns in which there is a company plant, an investment center for the company's stock, or the headquarters of a subsidiary company, the CEO would be welcomed as the subject of an interview by the local paper's financial editor.

The broadcast media should also be a high priority for executive contact. By working closely with public relations professionals, the CEO can gain access to millions of viewers and listeners of TV and radio news and talk shows. While broadcast news has a reputation for poor business coverage, a close examination of the news mix on any station will reveal a great many stories with business, financial, or economic implications. To a large extent, the poor representation of the businessman's perspective is a result of executives' reluctance to make themselves available to the broadcast media. If CEOs make themselves available to these media on a continuing basis, they will be heard.

The Executive as a Community Spokesperson

The CEO should address local civic, service, and social groups on matters affecting the firm and the community. In recent years, community groups have been active and vocal in their objections to corporate activities. An uninformed public can create major barriers for a company in a great many situations, including plant expansions, layoffs or plant closings, research and development, waste disposal, and pollution control. An active and visible CEO can educate the community and thereby convert it from a potential antagonist to a full partner in the efforts of the company.

IMPROVING EXECUTIVE PRESENTATIONS

The most frustrating experience for any public relations director occurs when "the boss flubs a speech." The points discussed in this chapter—convincing executives to speak out, planning a program, developing communications opportunities—all involve considerable effort by the public relations staff. When the executive handles the presentation poorly, that effort is wasted, and the message that was to be communicated may be lost. Like many other corporate problems, this can create an opportunity for PR directors. It calls attention to the need for careful preparation of executives for interviews, speeches, and broadcast appearances.

In rising to the top, most executives have had a great deal of experience making business presentations. In fact, top-notch presentation skills rank high on almost any list of executive qualifications. But some executives have not had the opportunity to do a great deal of public speaking and have not had much experience dealing with the media. This lack of experience can be disastrous in a communications effort. Consider, for example, the CEO whose eyes shift from camera to camera, because he doesn't know where to look during a TV interview. That may sound like a minor problem, but it can translate into a critical loss of credibility if the CEO is being interviewed about the possibility of a plant closing.

Training Programs

Public relations directors must see that executives have the skills they need to handle presentations well. Unfortunately, many executives are not aware that they need help and probably don't even know that it's available. In fact, it sometimes seems that the poorer an executive's presentation skills are, the more reluctant his staff is to suggest help. The public relations professional must broach the subject of training programs in such a way that it meets with enthusiastic executive response. Everyone is somewhat uncomfortable in the "spotlight," even the professionals, and, if handled properly, most executives will acknowledge the value of professional help.

A number of programs are available, and there are many similarities among them. When evaluating a program for the company, the public relations director should consider the following:

1. Content. Is it aimed at CEOs or at beauty pageant contestants? Get a program that is right for the circumstances.
2. Length. Does it give the executive a meaningful learning experience within a compact time frame? One day of intensive training should suffice.
3. Realism. There is no substitute for real studio conditions, working reporters, and trained instructors. A good training program should give the executive the chance to make mistakes in front of a "practice" camera. Those mistakes will improve the results when it counts.
4. Fundamentals. Be sure the training is grounded in sound public relations concepts. Successful interviews involve a great deal more than wearing the right color suit.

5. Tailoring. Custom-designed programs are often more expensive but they're worth the difference. Don't force senior executives to attend pre-packaged programs, where they sit with junior people from other companies and learn to smile.

The careful selection of a good training program for media interviews will pay off for the public relations director. A well-trained executive will relax and enjoy interviews. That executive will become an enthusiastic participant in a carefully planned program of executive communications.

Preparation of executives basically falls into two categories: improving basic group communications skills, and training for radio and television interviews.

Group Presentations

Whether the executive is addressing a small group from a local club or hundreds of shareholders at an annual meeting, his or her personal presentation skills have a major effect on the success of the communication. The audience may have already formed ideas about the company and its executives before seeing them in person. The first impressions can even further affect audience conceptions, which are based on clothing, style, body language, facial mannerisms, and so on.

There are several techniques that can quickly improve personal presentation skills. Before any presentation, the PR director can help with the following aspects.

1. *Preparation.* Familiarity with the material is the prerequisite to any successful personal presentation. Senior executives often fail, ironically, because they are poorly prepared. The classic example is the chief financial officer who knows the numbers, but who has a lot of trouble with the words on the day of the presentation.

2. *Participation.* Emphasize to your executives that a group presentation is not an "us vs. them" situation, but rather an opportunity to interact with the other people in the room. Through a variety of techniques, such as body motion, eye contact, and gestur-

ing, the executive can work to share an experience with the group, instead of merely presenting information to it.

3. *Materials.* The PR director can make an important contribution by supplying presentation materials that are carefully prepared. Speeches, for example, should be typed triple spaced with large type, and pages should not be stapled together. Everything the executive will need should be there and in good condition. In general, act as an "advance man."

4. *Follow-up.* Executives will learn that each presentation is different and that their ability to make the same points will vary from situation to situation. The PR director can help assure that the objectives of the meeting are met by distributing follow-up materials to meeting participants. Such materials can emphasize key points, summarize audience response, and clear up any misunderstanding that might have emerged during the meeting.

Careful planning that takes into account the above factors will contribute to the success of any program. Keep in mind that executives generally consider public presentations to be interruptions from their daily routine. The PR director must therefore take charge of the planning, the meeting content, and the follow-up.

Radio and Television Interviews

Although interviews for broadcast media hold much in common with face-to-face meetings, they have specific qualities that merit separate consideration. The characteristics that are unique to broadcast media, especially to television, can be pitfalls if the executive is unprepared for them. Tension and confusion can result, creating a barrier to communication.

A broadcast interview or conversation strives to create the illusion of a spontaneous interchange of ideas, yet at the same time it must be structured well enough to make sense and make points in some logical sequence. While it demands informality it is still a performance of sorts—an artificial reconstruction of an interview.

It is inappropriate for the guest to use scripts or notes, or to memorize lines or speeches—these techniques destroy the illusion of spontaneity. The manner and style of the executive can make a stronger impression than the subject matter. The elements of artificiality inherent in a broadcast situation are all factors that can hinder the presentation of the product, company, or program. In addition, the executive sees, at first, a veritable jungle of cables, microphones, lights, and cameras populated by a busy crew. Even the most articulate spokesperson would be inhibited in such surroundings. However, once the executive knows what to expect and how to behave in this unique medium, these elements will cease to be barriers to communication. Instead, they will all become part of the means to communication.

OBJECTIVE-ORIENTED INTERVIEWS

By setting an objective and then working to achieve it, executives can vastly improve their broadcast interview abilities. The host, or reporter, has only one objective—maintaining viewer interest. In many instances a talk show host, for example, may not be interested in what you have to say. As a professional, the host has learned to be aware of a number of other things (such as time and station breaks) while appearing to concentrate on the guest.

The executive's role in a radio or television interview is that of an expert who has come to share expertise with the audience. The executive will be comfortable in that role, and can use it as a vehicle to achieve the objectives set for the interview.

PACING INTERVIEWS

"Pacing" is broadcast jargon. A well-paced segment keeps moving, is interesting, and brings home a single point well. Once an executive knows the rules of the game, interviews can provide the company with an opportunity to use pacing to achieve important communications objectives. The public relations director should give executives the following guidelines to follow:

1. Speak in personal terms. Say "I" not "we." This is contrary to everything a good executive learns about teamwork, but it improves the credibility and directness of responses.

2. Be accurate, even if it hurts. Never exaggerate and never, never lie. Say "I don't know," if that's the case, and promise to find out. Never repeat offensive questions, even to deny them.
3. Be careful. No response is "off the record" in a radio or TV interview. If you don't want to be quoted as saying something, don't say it.
4. Empathize with the audience. To be successful on television, a spokesperson must be exciting, and the only way to be exciting is to approach the material from the audience's point of view.
5. Get to the point quickly. Answer a question in 10 words or less. When given the opportunity, amplify in 100 words or less. This also contradicts the business executive's way of thinking. An executive will generally begin an answer by reviewing the background and then make the point. In broadcast interviews, that executive must make the point *first,* then follow with the background.

SUMMARY

Corporate executives are clearly operating in a difficult environment for effective communications. Their credibility is low, the business environment is complex, and the press is, at best, skeptical. However, the executive can play an important role in corporate communications, as a spokesperson, as a news source, and as a member of the community. Properly trained, the top executive will become an able and willing member of the corporate communications team.

12: Growing Pains
for Investor Relations

ALTHOUGH investor relations (IR) has been a significant part of communications at large corporations and agencies for many years, its emergence as a specialized function is of comparatively recent origin. The emphasis on investor relations, along with great changes within the investor relations target audiences, has brought growing pains to the profession. These have made the lot of the manager much more difficult. Never perhaps in business history has such a young developing profession had to cope with such sweeping changes, challenges, and responsibilities.

The catchall nature of the responsibilities is one of the challenges facing the IR manager. The investor relations professional must have sound personal and mass communications skills; a knowledge of finance, accounting, economics, financial analysis, and securities law; and an understanding of the securities marketplace.

One frequent problem is that people entering the profession are often skilled in only a few critical areas rather than in all of them. The public relations executive, for example, may possess outstanding communications skills yet be weak in understanding the securities marketplace, financial analysis, or other topics. Conversely, the finance manager may be able to speak the language of Wall Street to the right people but lack the communications skills to turn his efforts into professional mass communications. The broker or analyst recruited by the corporation as IR manager may understand the securities industry in depth but lack communications skills and corporate background.

The membership roster of the National Investor Relations Institute (NIRI) shows the diverse backgrounds of IR professionals today. The roster is segmented almost evenly among individuals with job titles in finance, public relations or communications, public relations counsel, and, finally, investor relations. Those who hold IR titles have various backgrounds, from security analysis to public relations to finance to education.

It is essential that IR people, and the managers who oversee their function, have a working knowledge of the entire field. Such rounding out is one of the principal goals of this chapter. No attempt will be made to deal with subjects in depth, but the coverage will be comprehensive enough to provide a good overview of such topics as the changing nature of investor relations, communications techniques, investor relations from the perspective of various audiences, and communications trends, budgeting, and controls.

THE CHANGING NATURE OF INVESTOR RELATIONS

Few business people have as many opportunities to learn about the changes taking place in their professions as the investor relations professional does. He has a regular offering each year of seminars sponsored by NIRI, Financial Analysts Federation (FAF), and a host of other financial publications and financial services suppliers. The proliferation of these events indicates little shortage of subject matter. The profession, obviously, is attempting to meet the challenge of a rapidly changing environment.

Those changes have largely taken place in two areas: the framework in which investor relations operates and the communications techniques it uses to adapt to the changing framework. The framework has changed in that the traditional audiences for investor relations efforts are smaller and their composition is different. This has resulted in active competition among companies to attract the attention of these audiences.

Wall Street Consolidation

There has been a continuing wave of consolidations among brokerage firms. To some, the consolidation implies a fundamental sickness in the securities industry, the forerunner to an industry controlled by a few strong firms. To others, the consolidation is viewed as a healthy reduction of a previously inefficient, bloated industry. No matter which side of the fence the IR manager sits on regarding this issue, the final result is that the consolidation has left him an audience that is reduced in size and expanded in work load.

Dwindling Research Capabilities

The consolidations and the dwindling research capabilities have, of course, had their effect. In the past, a corporate investor relations person could establish contact with 10 or 20 Wall Street analysts and feed them information. The analysts then did their legwork and analysis and passed the word along to scores of their institutional counterparts. This was a quick way for the corporate IR to spread the word throughout the investment community. This no longer works because many of the institutional brokerage firms have gone out of business and there are far fewer analysts.

Emergence of National Market System

A key component of the National Market System is the composite quote system (CQS). Basically, this means that the investment professionals, including brokers, traders, and analysts, will have immediate access to bid and ask prices for a given company on all exchanges where the company's stock is traded. This means that the specialists in a company's stock on, say, the New York Stock Exchange, the Midwest Stock Exchange, and the Philadelphia-Baltimore-Washington Exchange will be in price competition with each other as well as with the market makers—or traders—in the over-the-counter market.

The end result of the new National Market System will be increased competition among companies for attention by the market makers. The market makers will go where the action is (i.e., high volume, quality stocks), while more lackluster issues surely will suffer from lack of attention.

Thus, the advent of the National Market System will bring to the trading community the same competition IR people have experienced in getting their messages across to analysts and brokers.

Institutional Dominance

Another well-documented factor contributing to the competitive IR environment, as institutions continue increasing their trading volume, is the declining importance of the individual investor. Institutions have talked more and more about broadening their portfolios to meet the prudent man requirements imposed by the Employee Retirement Income Security Act (ERISA). This broadening, however, does not appear to apply to the common stock portfolio. *Broadening,* apparently, simply means a lot more emphasis on fixed income securities.

Competition—A Summary

In summary, then, the IR manager faces fewer analysts, fewer brokerage firms, and a greater emphasis on investments other than common stocks. At the same time, he faces institutions that are beefing up fixed income investments and continuing to limit common stock purchases to a few select companies.

It's not the brightest picture in the world. But some companies are operating highly successful programs within it.

NEGOTIATING THE COMPETITIVE ENVIRONMENT

Broadly speaking, successful IR programs are beating the competitive environment in three ways.

Heavier Emphasis on Personal Communications

Not too many years ago, the IR effort was one of mass communications. Companies judged success by the number of annual reports distributed, the size of their mailing lists, and the number of huge formal analysts society presentations made. Today, the successful IR programs lean more toward quality than quantity. A broad mailing list and formal society presentations still have their places in the corporate IR effort, but increasingly, the real results are being achieved on a personal level.

The IR professional builds a core following of financial decisionmakers through a cultivation process that assures complete and in-depth understanding of the company by a group of key analysts. He also develops a cadre of brokers close enough to the company to effectively market it as an investment. And he continually updates these two groups through personal contact.

The personal approach is reflected in many ways: the growing number of one-on-one and small group meetings with analysts and brokers; the telephone alert to key members of the financial community as material news breaks; and the personal meetings between management and large shareholders as management travels.

Selling To and Through

An outgrowth of the personal communications approach to IR is what is called "selling to and through" the brokerage firm or institution. IR efforts used to start and end with the analysts. Now, IR professionals are increasingly merchandising the analyst contact into other areas of the brokerage firm or institution. If the analyst is assured of your creditability, even if he's not made a recommendation on your stock, he's usually quite willing to set up a meeting with the broker sales force or with traders in his firm. On the institutional side, successful work with the analyst can be merchandised to the portfolio manager. By doing this, the IR manager assures that his messages are reaching the people that actually move the stock rather than relying totally on the overworked analyst to do this job. The key ingredient, however, is primary contact with the appropriate analyst.

Specialized Approach

Another result of expanded personal communications is that IR people are learning that there's really no such thing as a retail stock, an institutional stock, a high flier, or a dog. If you pick and choose your audience carefully enough, any well-run company can offer certain attractions to certain investors. The key to successful IR is getting to those audiences and finding out what they, as investors, are looking for.

For example, it's widely believed that regional brokerage firms prefer to follow companies located in their geographical area. But a survey of such firms conducted by Ketchum MacLeod & Grove Public Relations in early 1977[1] found such provincialism was not the case. The research directors who were interviewed said they would follow any good prospect regardless of location. The most important factor is whether or not your company fits the firm's interests. For example, does the firm concentrate on stocks in certain industries?

Another investment criterion is size. Many firms with smaller floats do not think they have a chance with the institutions. We worked with a company that was trying to attract the interest of Sears Profit Sharing Trust but didn't meet the high float requirements of this gigantic fund. A little homework, however, revealed that the same industry analyst who worked for the trust also did analysis for Sears Bank, which had much less sizable float requirements. Even the huge investment companies frequently have select subfunds where a low-float stock can be welcome. And bank trust departments, as revealed in the Ketchum MacLeod & Grove survey, have few arbitrary cutoff points for investment.

The importance of homework can't be overstated. The difference between fruitless and fruitful IR field trips may be determined by whether or not you see the right people. The firms to contact are those whose investment criteria match the investment attributes of your company. In evaluating a brokerage firm, you can use the directories listed later in this chapter and the telephone to find out whether or not your company will fit with the firm's interests. Issues to consider are:

Orientation—Is it retail or institutional?

Branch offices—Are there any near your plant or office locations?

Number of analysts—How strong is research capability; how much analysis is really done by brokers?

Number of brokers—What is their retail strength?

Specialists—Are any in your industry?

Correspondence house—Where does the firm buy research on the outside?

Market makers—Is the firm making a market in your stock (even though research might not be following it)?

Research superstars—Who are the people you really should see because their opinion carries a lot of weight even outside the firm?

INVESTOR RELATIONS AUDIENCES

In addition to matching the investment attractions of his company to the investment criteria of the target brokerage firm or institution, a successful IR manager must also match his information dissemination practices to the information needs of various types of financial professionals.

Analysts

Despite the occasional flurries of publicity about the growing number of technical analysts who play the market based on everything from macroeconomics to the position of the planets, fundamental analysis techniques still prevail.

Fundamentalists are looking for depth and detail of corporate information, according to FAF's Russ Mason.[2] He cites the 10-K, the 10-Q, the annual report, and financial publicity as basic materials to be given to the fundamentalists. Form 10-K, the company's annual financial report filed with the Securities and Exchange Commission, and form 10-Q, the quarterly report filed with the SEC, both answer questions required by law and do not necessarily include the same information as the annual report to stockholders.

Mason's comments are generally substantiated by Ketchum MacLeod & Grove research of regional brokerage firms.[3] Aside from personal contact with the chief executive and financial vice president, we found the most popular types of communication to be the form 10-K, the annual report, and particularly, as the number of analysts dwindle, financial fact books. Of lesser importance—but nonetheless significant—to the in-depth study of a company are such tools as news releases, publicity in the business press, and corporate advertising.

Mason also points to an upswing in generalists, as opposed to specialists. He estimates that no more than 20 percent of FAF membership represent specialists, and these are concentrated primarily in big firms in large cities. Although the information needs of the generalist and specialist are essentially the same, Mason cautions the IR manager to make sure he starts "further back" with the generalist, because the generalist will not have the same industry background the specialist has.[4]

Brokers

Although the analyst is looking for all the in-depth information he can obtain, the broker's main needs are simplicity and clarity. Frequently, the broker has only a minute or two on the telephone to convince his client that XYZ company is a good buy. If the story or company is complicated, the pitch is that much less effective. Thus, for communications aimed at brokers, your company and its performance must be positioned succinctly and clearly. This is particularly true for the annual report, which, according to our survey, is the broker's key selling tool.

Another concern of the broker is timeliness, or more appropriately stated, timely visibility. His job is a lot easier if he can say to his client, "Did you see in the *Journal* where XYZ's third quarter is down a nickel a share? Well, I've got the full press release in my hands, and the CEO says that order backlog for the next quarter is up substantially. I think they might be looking at a record year, despite the blip last quarter. If I were you, I'd buy now." The broker who can start out his sales call by asking the client if he's seen a certain business periodical article or corporate ad about a company saves valuable time in positioning the company and can get right to the meat of his pitch.

Portfolio Managers

The information needs of the portfolio manager probably lie somewhere between the analyst's need for depth and the broker's need for quick positioning and timely access. One way of meeting these needs was related by Roger Beidler, vice president, investor relations, of Koppers Company.

In a recent annual report, Koppers prepared a highly unique combination of the 10-K and annual report in an effort to reach institutional investors and professional money managers. In the front of the report, the company printed a simplified summary section of about seven pages, aimed primarily at brokers. The response of the portfolio managers to the summary section was unexpectedly good.

Traders

When viewed in the context of a National Market System, the trader becomes an increasingly important IR audience. OTC companies have long recognized the need to address their market makers, but listed companies, which have dealt with their exchange specialists all along, have regarded the third-market trader largely as an enigma.

As Ketchum MacLeod & Grove reported in a discussion piece on the trading community in late 1978, "timing isn't everything to the trader, it's the *only* thing." [5] By communicating quickly to the trader as material news breaks on Dow Jones, you can avoid the wide fluctuations in stock price that can arise when one market maker has access to or knowledge of information another has not yet seen. Other than access to relevant news, the trader needs or wants very little by way of communications. Meetings after the close of the market, along with annual and quarterly report mailings, should be sufficient. A key communications tool here is to know what types of data traders want, and then set up this component of your IR program accordingly.

Underwriters

A company's lead underwriter or investment banker is frequently close to top management. Senior members of investment banking firms typically sit on corporate boards of directors. However, most IR programs ignore potential participating underwriters as a group. Yet participating underwriters may determine whether a public stock or bond offering is fully subscribed. Failure to have a fully subscribed issue can mean less capital than anticipated in an equity offering or a higher effective interest rate on what turns out to be a discounted bond offering. Supplying participating underwriters with enough information to make an intelligent judgment about the company is the responsibility of the IR program. If you want to reach the underwriter, you should take your message directly to him.

Underwriters can be important allies in the IR effort. Some lead underwriters walk away from a company after the issue has been subscribed. The result is that a secondary market for the stock may not develop and the price may plummet. Others, however, like to stay close to the company, partly out of a sense of service, but mostly with the idea that future business will result. These individuals can be helpful in developing the IR program and in setting up periodic meetings for management.

INVESTMENT CRITERIA

Probably the best place to start in considering investment criteria is to put yourself in the shoes of the analyst broker or the portfolio manager. His question will be: "Can I make money on this company?" Making money is related to:

Liquidity—Can I turn my paper profit into a real one quickly?
Industry prospects—Is the company in a growth industry?
Company prospects—What are the company's growth prospects?
  Is it adequately capitalized to realize those prospects? Is the
  company on sound financial footing?

Marketability—How marketable is the company? Is it in a topical, exciting business? Is it visible? Does it lead its industry?

Particular types of financial institutions have particular interests. Following are some generalizations that have been developed from research studies and from discussions with individuals employed in these areas.

Brokerage Firms

A report on our study of 37 leading regional brokerage firms[6] noted: "Most research heads said they would follow any company they believe has good investment potential, regardless of its size, location or other considerations. Of those analysts having 'cut-off' points on the size of a company they will follow, about a half dozen pointed to annual sales levels ranging from $50 million to $300 million. A few others required a minimum level of earnings—from $1 million to $7 million."

Only 3 of the 37 analysts interviewed said float was a consideration. Most analysts reported that brokers in their firms follow their research recommendations closely. Brokers, according to the study, start with the firm's researched companies but pick from among those on the basis of "marketability."

Banks

As mentioned earlier, in a survey of the nation's top 100 banks,[7] we found that banks had few arbitrary cutoff points for the approved lists. To be more specific, nearly half of the banks responding reported no cutoffs. The others, which have statistical considerations, usually cited float, capitalization, and minority ownership. Looking more closely, we found, "almost without exception, a solid company with $100 million in capitalization, a float of 2 million shares and limited minority ownership should have no problems with arbitrary cutoffs."

Mutual Funds

Generalizing about mutual funds is like trying to generalize about fast food emporiums. According to *Business Week,* there are 700 or so mutual funds offering something for everyone. The ones that are doing well today, reports *Business Week,* are diversifying into such varied investments as municipal bonds, options, indexing, and gems.[8] In this milieu, the IR manager has a heavy selection job to do. We recommend starting with the Vickers report to find out which mutual funds already hold stock in your company and then calling those funds to find out what criteria they're using. Match these criteria to those of the new firms you're interested in attracting to see which are working off the same formula.

THE INDIVIDUAL INVESTORS

Although much of the attention in IR programs is directed to professionals, the end objectives are frequently stated in terms of attracting more individual participation. This parallels attempts in other areas of public relations to get messages across to the general public through the mass media.

Individual participation is desirable for many companies, because individuals provide a stabilizing counterbalance to the often fickle institutions, are usually supportive of management, and are frequently investors for the long haul. But all too often, efforts to reach them are frustrating. This is difficult to comprehend, considering the frequency of shareholder communications required by law and exchange regulations. Each year, most shareholders receive:

The annual report
Three quarterlies
Proxy notice and card
Opportunities to attend the annual meeting

In addition, standard IR tools in most programs include:

Annual meeting speech reprint mailing
Reprints of news articles, ads, and other timely information
Key news releases

Yet, for some reason, little of this appears to be getting through. One reason managers may be failing is that they are underestimating the intelligence of their audience. As a group individual investors are well educated (65 percent have attended or graduated from college), hold responsible positions often related to some facet of the business world (nearly half are professional, technical, managerial, or sales people), and have savings income to invest.[9] While the "little old lady in tennis shoes" may still exist, she's probably a lot more sophisticated about investments than many people believe.

Another reason shareholder communications fail to do their job is that too often they suffer from committee editing. This was pointed out in a *Public Relations Journal* article in August 1978 concerning the successful internal management of the annual report. The article notes that one individual can develop a strong, communicative annual report concept, but the concept frequently is destroyed by the sheer numbers of managers who fight to protect their special interests or directions.[10]

Companies that invest in expensive surveys frequently seek quick demographic profiles of shareholders rather than the underlying reasons for their interests. Good research is as important for shareholder communications as it is for professional investor relations.

A Marketing Approach

For the IR manager, the solutions start with a marketing approach to the problem. Shareholders and potential shareholders are like consumers and potential consumers: They're skeptical, reasonably easily bored, and want to know what's in it for them.

They're also sophisticated. And they may be motivated to buy your stock through a number of different attractions.

The key to successful management of the IR function is to put to work the shareholder communications tools that already exist. The annual meeting, so often a mere formality, can be enhanced by including plant tours and promoted through additional shareholder mailings. Quarterly meetings can be scheduled near concentrations of shareholders.

The annual report very often is designed to be too many things to too many people and loses everyone in the process. It should be viewed for its primary purpose—shareholder communications.

Investors can be updated, as the professional investment community is, through news releases, business articles, or publicity mailings. Corporate publicity efforts can recognize shareholder concentrations, and interviews with local business editors can be scheduled accordingly.

The shareholder wants to feel that he's part of the inner circle of people who know what's going on. He wants to read corporate literature only once and not be forced to sift through all the corporate jargon that often permeates these reports. It's a fairly simple order. But frequently, it will mean changing the old ways of doing things. And that, for the manager, is the challenge.

SETTING OBJECTIVES

Most of the communications tools of investor relations are outlined in the chapter on financial communications and in other literature. The tools will work best if they are in the framework of a program with measurable objectives and defined audiences.

As an IR manager, you may be charged with "getting the stock price up" or increasing trading volume. If you agree to these, you're guaranteed to keep your job in bull markets. In a declining market, however, you may be stranded on third base.

As with any communications effort, the only true measure of an IR program is through scientific research to gauge your success in meeting more specific and measurable objectives. Fortunately, quality research in IR is frequently cheaper than it is with other audiences because the universe is smaller. Objectives like these can be measured by research:

Increase analysts following the company by 20 percent.

Obtain 95 percent confidence level among key analysts as to credibility and timeliness of company communications.

Achieve 50 percent awareness level among individual shareholders about the company's new product line.

The successful manager knows he cannot afford to ignore any audience. Investor relations audiences are like a chain. If one link is broken, whether at the level of the analyst, portfolio manager or broker, or individual investor, the results for the whole program will not be as good as they could have been.

SETTING UP AN IR DEPARTMENT

Staffing

The first question you'll probably ask yourself if you're starting an IR department from scratch is who will manage it. Before you determine the answer, you'll have to ask three other questions:

1. What are the strengths of the rest of the IR team? By asking this question you can decide whether to go after the financial PR professional (if your staff is weak in this area), the finance professional (if your PR staff handles financial communications completely and well), or the person out of a brokerage house (if you feel uncomfortable with the company's knowledge of what the audience wants).

2. What will the main duties of the function be? If it's primarily contact work, the person from a brokerage firm would be a good selection. On the other hand, if the main function is producing financial literature and communications, the financial PR pro would be right.

3. How much can I pay? IR salaries are steep when compared with most PR slots.

Reporting

In establishing the IR function, a primary decision is determining to whom it should report. The answer is concerned with effectiveness. Programs are ineffective because of one of three managerial problems:

1. The manager or his boss does not have clout. He spends too much time negotiating the streams of corporate politics, being polite to everyone, and, as a result, doesn't get anything done.

2. The manager may have full clout, but top management does not support the function. Top management involvement is indispensable to the successful IR effort. "I heard it straight from the horse's mouth," is probably one of the most important phrases the broker or analyst can use. The executive whose involvement makes that phrase possible will reap the rewards.

3. The budget is insufficient. In this case, sufficient becomes relative. The best way to decide if your budget is sufficient is to go back to your audiences and determine if all are being covered and if you're covering them with enough frequency to meet objectives.

The question of where the IR function reports is secondary to making sure it will be effective. The 1978 PRSA investor relations section survey cited earlier provides some insight into what other companies are doing. It reports that over one-third of its members report to the CEO, while a slightly smaller number report to the PR or public affairs VP. Another 10 percent report to the president or a corporate secretary.

Support

By its very nature, the fledgling or established IR department depends on the rest of the corporation for much of its ammunition. In staffing and reporting, it's critical to establish smooth working relationships from the beginning with the following groups in and outside the company:

Top management
Public relations and PR counsel

Finance department and outside auditors
Legal department and outside legal counsel

Beyond these groups, there's also a need for the periodic involvement of manufacturing and marketing executives, both for information and for visibility that demonstrates management depth.

A *Library of Tools*
The homework so essential in doing a successful IR job requires a substantial library of publications. Some key references are:

Financial Analysts Federation Directory—lists all FAF members by city and firm affiliation and specialty.
Vickers Guide to Investment Company Portfolios— lists which funds hold what stocks.
The E-Z Telephone Directory of Brokers and Banks—lists all stockbrokers and banks in the New York area.
Security Dealers of North America—the industry "red book," covers all brokerage firm branches and their firm's business concentration.
NYSE Guide—lists requirements for New York Stock Exchange Listed Companies along with SEC requirements.
Amec Guide—lists requirements for American Stock Exchange Listed Companies.
Institutions—lists key individuals, portfolio size, and other key facts for institutions.

The most helpful periodicals include:

Institutional Investor—bible of the institutional firms.
FAF Journal
Financial Executives—magazine of the Financial Executives Institute.
NIRI notes—magazine of National Investor Relations Institute.
Wall Street Transcript—a complete digest of analysts presentations, earnings releases, and the like.
IR Newsletter—PRSA IR section newsletter.

Wall Street Letter—published by *Institutional Investor,* indicates current events on Wall Street.

Professional Organizations

Membership and seminar attendance within several organizations can be helpful. At the forefront is the National Investor Relations Institute. Other groups where IR topics frequently are addressed include the Public Relations Society of America, Financial Analysts Federation, and Financial Executives Institute.

IN SUMMARY

In this discussion of investor relations, six facts are salient:

1. The IR profession is young and growing. As such, management should recognize the size of the challenge it faces.
2. IR professionals face a fast-changing, harsh, and competitive environment. Their audience is shrinking, and its very viability is at stake.
3. The changes and the environment can be addressed, provided homework and selective positioning are accomplished.
4. The IR audiences have special information needs that vary according to each audience's own business.
5. Attracting individual investors is probably the key challenge for the IR manager.
6. A marketing approach is called for with all audiences.

REFERENCES
1. *Investor Relations in Major Commercial Banks.*
2. Personal communication, November 4, 1978.
3. *Investor Relations in Regional Money Centers.*
4. Personal communication, November 4, 1978.
5. *Investor Relations with the Trader* (Pittsburgh, Pa.: Ketchum MacLeod & Grove/Botsford Ketchum Public Relations, 1978).
6. *Investor Relations in Regional Money Centers.*
7. *Investor Relations in Major Commercial Banks.*
8. "Mutual Funds: A Guide for Investors," *Business Week* (April 17, 1978).
9. New York Stock Exchange, *Shareownership,* 1975.
10. James Roop and Louis Capozzi, "Ten Ways to Fight Those Internal Battles."

13: Wading Through the Maze of Government Bureaucracy

THERE IS A SAYING that goes something like this: "Just when I had the game figured out, someone changed the rules." Many PR managers do feel the rules in today's complex business environment are being changed, and changed often. The rules are those established by government, at all levels—local, state, and federal. The pressures for government regulation of business are strong and, in the name of consumer, environmental, and economic protection, will probably increase.

Government sits as an almost invisible partner of every company. It takes its share of earnings through taxes; regulates product content, safety, labeling, and advertising; sets standards for hiring, firing, and working conditions; controls interaction with the environment and community; and even tells management what it can and cannot do politically to influence these potent factors.

To visualize the size and scope of the problem, look at what is happening in Washington: greater controls, more spending, chronic deficits, dubious effectiveness of many public programs, mounting intervention of private functions, and a gradual erosion of economic freedom. Washington observers say that even those who have traditionally sought an expanded government presence are having second thoughts. Perhaps it was this kind of reaction that led to the 1978 California taxpayers' rebellion and passage of the now famous Proposition 13. The California action has not solved the problem of a balanced budget nationally, and many still wonder, "Where will it all end?"

The most pressing question is, what can be done about it?

THE ROLE OF PUBLIC RELATIONS

A great deal can be done. An expanded role for public relations must be considered. To be sure, we are hearing such terms as *government relations, government affairs,* and *public affairs* nearly as much as *public relations.* No matter how you define these terms, however, they relate to an exchange of information. In the following pages, we will explore the reasons that communication with government should be part of your public relations program. Our discussion will focus primarily on Washington, but you will see a similarity of need and importance for state and local government functions.

In the past several years, the official Washington bureaucracy, with its numerous agencies and complex organizations, has greatly expanded in size and in its influence on business. The problems of communicating in Washington have been compounded by the tremendous growth of staff. Although the number of congressmen and senators has remained approximately the same for several decades, congressional staff sizes have exploded. Today, 30,000 people are directly involved in the legislative process.

Numbers are important, but they by no means tell the whole story. The complexities of modern American life have caused Congress to pass broad legislation that requires interpretation and regulation by the executive branch. Since 1970, more than 20 new federal regulatory agencies have been formed under such laws. These agencies, which have a profound effect on business, include the Consumer Product Safety Commission, the Environmental Protection Agency, the Farm Credit Administration, the International Trade Commission, the National Transportation Safety Board, the Nuclear Regulatory Commission, and others incorporated into the Department of Energy. As agencies grow, they tend to duplicate functions. It seems everyone is in, or wants to get into, the act.

The challenge confronting American business is complicated by public opinion, which holds it in low esteem. There was a time—

during World War II and the ensuing postwar years—when an outstanding leader of the business community was lionized in Washington. Today, he is more apt to encounter cynicism from many of those he contacts. Thus, improving public opinion is vitally important. Elected officials are more receptive to issues that have the support of their constituents.

A primary function of your public relations program should be to audit the level of contact your business has with government. Some key questions are: How well are you known to your congressional representatives? Do they, in fact, know what you do and the contribution you make to the community? What is your relationship with businesses similar to your own? Do you participate in mutually beneficial organizations and trade associations that can help you in time of need?

This information will be helpful in structuring an effective government relations program. The objective is to have friends who will support your position in Congress, regulatory agencies, and allied associations.

The most important element of a functioning, ongoing public relations program is how it is structured. Whether performed by outside counsel or by staff, the work must involve the top decisionmakers. Generally, the chief executive, rather than a lesser official, is required in meeting with key legislators and other Washington bureaucrats. For this reason, it is essential that the public relations activities, as they relate to government, be guided by the CEO.

FOUR KEY ACTIVITIES

The public relations function, insofar as Washington is concerned, should have four major components to be effective.

Lobbying

Lobbying means effective representation before Congress, regulatory agencies, and executive departments. Most businesses already have some form of representation, whether through their own government relations office in Washington or through a business association that maintains a staff to lobby on behalf of the membership. The lobby function is important both as a means of directly delivering your views on a specific piece of legislation or action by a regulatory agency and as an intelligence gathering and early warning network that can help to put out little "brush fires."

Grass Roots Support

There is no question that sound support at home can be enormously helpful. The members of Congress whose districts include your business and who represent your employees will be responsive to the needs and wishes of the constituency. The public relations program will be tremendously important both in creating the necessary visibility with the congressional representatives and in gaining the support of locally elected officials, your own employees, shareholders, suppliers, and the community. It was this kind of pressure created by business, labor, and other interests that finally moved Congress to take action on the oppressive rules and regulations of the Occupational Safety and Health Administration.

How to achieve this grass roots support is sometimes difficult to target. The public relations professionals should be totally involved in all activities that shape the image of your business, including employee communications, community affairs, and communications to shareholders and the financial and business press. Properly executed, all of these communications functions have a great effect on how the company is ultimately viewed.

Research and Policy Development

Corporations are still considered private entities in the sense that they are not government owned. But they are also perceived as social entities, that is, as organizations that must respond to public opinion and the public interest. The phrase "the public interest" is no longer measured strictly in economic terms. Subjective and qualitative considerations, ranging from public health to competitive practices, are also vitally important.

Government, particularly Washington, has the power to transform public demand—or perceived demand—whether or not it represents consensus, into binding law and regulation. For this reason, business leaders today must make themselves heard, but they must be armed with reliable, convincing data and supportable arguments. Business has now entered an era that requires candor and credibility, to stem the almost daily barrage of criticism mounted against it. Business cannot afford to maintain a low profile; corporate executives need to fulfill the role of "corporate statesmen," not simply react to public policies.

To accomplish this, the chief executive, through the public relations function, must be prepared to convey expert and factual information in terms government will respond to. A good example of this type of presentation is found in the case of the American automobile manufacturers. Every year both state and federal governments imposed new safety and environmental standards for automobiles. In the beginning, the industry leaders argued that they could not meet the deadlines and that it would be too costly for them to accomplish the task. While these statements were most likely true, they lacked the perspective of what is "in the public interest." When the auto industry began talking in terms of increased car prices, fewer jobs, and other adverse effects on the public, it found Congress and some state governments much more willing to listen.

Public relations counsel can be helpful in identifying the areas where research on specific issues should be undertaken. This function should be ongoing and not simply used when a crisis occurs. To be successful, the research must be aimed at developing positions that will inform and educate people about your business, telling what you are doing and what problems you face.

The positions developed through these activities will be appropriate for speeches and for communication with specific target audiences. Over a period of time, such communication forms a firm base from which to effectively respond to challenges from the government.

Political Action

There can be no substitute for financial contributions to candidates and personal efforts to get out the vote. For business, these are aimed at electing people to public office who understand that profit is not a four-letter word.

Corporations cannot make direct contributions, but they can encourage individuals to contribute. In recent years, many companies have developed political action committees known as PACs. However, even with the increase in business PACs, the business community as a whole is still far behind the unions when it comes to political action, indicating that much more can be accomplished.

As part of a government affairs program, key employees should be informed of the importance of the PAC and how to support it.

STATE AND LOCAL GOVERNMENT

It is very important to establish a government affairs program at the local level. Government at the national level sets all types of rules and regulations regarding health, the environment, and the economy, but governments closer to home have a real impact, also. Land-use planning, availability of water and other necessary energy resources, housing for employees, and taxation are increasingly concerns that must be handled through local and state governments. In light of Proposition 13 in California, there no doubt will be increasing interest in Washington in returning functions to the states and in turn to the local communities.

Top management needs to be involved in local issues. This often is best accomplished with the aid of competent public relations counsel. No matter how the corporation is structured, the public relations function, as it relates to involvement with government at any level, must answer directly to the chief executive.

Considering the current mood of Washington, it is important to evaluate your present contact with government and to chart your future actions.

NINE GUIDELINES FOR A SOUND PROGRAM

As an aid to developing a sound government relations program, we cite nine guidelines. These apply whether the program is carried out as an in-house capability or with the help of knowledgeable outside counsel.

1. Find out the motivations, missions, and interests of the officials with whom you are dealing, in an effort to anticipate their responses and possible actions.

2. Present a candid case for your position. Good public relations counsel will help you avoid the pitfalls of ignoring opposing views, making misstatements or overstatements, and withholding pertinent facts.

3. Prepare background papers for press aides or staff.

4. Establish contacts with lower-echelon staff and aides. Your chief executive can talk with congressmen and cabinet-level officials, but don't overlook the importance of establishing contacts with those who actually prepare analyses of legislation or write the briefs on rules and regulations.

5. Follow up initial contacts. Government officials can be expected to be skeptical. After all, they can be held accountable for decisions and actions.

6. Supply officials with candid and credible information as a routine function of your ongoing public relations effort. Relevant documentation, statistics, and other research information may already be on hand as a normal function of the program.

7. Make your individual company voice heard, even though you may already be a part of a trade association that is active in lobbying. Remember the association's message is a consensus of the entire industry—not yours alone.

8. When approaching state and national legislators on a particular issue, strengthen your position with grass roots support from highly credible constituents.

9. Treat all communications as public information when dealing

with government. Public relations counsel can help assure accuracy in the interpretation of your views.

The complexities of government and the need for candid and open communication require every progressive corporation to have a solid plan and program for communications. Although it is not necessary to subscribe to all the recommendations offered here, a comprehensive government relations program is becoming more and more critical to meet the growing number of regulations.

14: Communicating the Consumer Affairs Program

ACTIONS TO INCREASE the public's confidence in a company, its products, and its policies represent the consumer affairs concern of the company. Their importance is obvious, because lack of consumer confidence has precipitated many of the government regulations discussed in the preceding chapter.

"Getting out the news" of various consumer activities and developments is an important function of the public relations profession. Beyond that, public relations has an important role in recommending to top management other means of creating public interest in the company. The PR professional must inform management what the public needs to know that will increase its trust in the company.

This chapter is mainly concerned with helping the public relations manager who is assuming direction of consumer affairs communications. We will seek to explain the problems and obstacles as well as to point out the contributions such managers can make to public understanding and trust on behalf of their companies.

OBSTACLES AND OPPORTUNITIES

The Increase in Skepticism

There is justifiable concern about the ability of contemporary business management to gain the confidence of the public. Some recent disclosures indicate that this challenge is formidable.

In 1980, U.S. industry spent an estimated $43 billion dollars, most of it in television advertising, to persuade people to buy its goods or services. That amount is about half as much as business is estimated to have spent this year to comply with government regulations. It is slightly less than half of the $95 billion that business invested in new plant and equipment in 1979.

Considering the size of the expenditures, American business should enjoy favorable public opinion about its products and policies. Two statistics from a recent survey indicate this is not so. The survey asked Americans to evaluate nine institutions whose activities are crucial to individual and national prosperity, health, security, and general well-being. These institutions were banks, big business, churches, Congress, labor unions, the military complex, public schools, the Supreme Court, and television. Those surveyed were asked to indicate the institutions in which they had a high degree of trust. Only 27 percent had that amount of trust in big business. Television ranked even lower, with only 21 percent.

Obviously, current consumer confidence in big business, and the principal communications medium it uses, appears to be in pretty sorry shape. At the same time, American consumers are wary of entrusting government to set the standards for the products they buy. In recent years, there has been strong resistance in Congress to any further broadening of the powers of agencies to regulate product standards.

It is evident that the public is suspicious not only of corporate activities but also of federal or other regulatory programs that would be a "big brother" check on those activities. A program of communicating consumer affairs activities cannot succeed if those responsible for it fail to understand the main reasons for these negative public attitudes.

The question that arises is: Why the low marks for an economic system that has brought high material comforts and expanding lifestyle opportunities to most people?

The Background of Discontent

The proven ability of the free enterprise system to produce an abundant life for many also has created accompanying complexities. Those planning a consumer affairs communications program must face this fact. The increasing number of new products and services has almost as many negative effects as positive ones. Many new products are difficult to evaluate for their total service capabilities and product life and are even harder to repair. The problem becomes more acute because it is difficult to find someone who will repair a malfunctioning product and the charges may exceed the original cost of the product. The new population mobility has added to the confusion. A product purchased in Topeka cannot always be exchanged or repaired if it breaks down in Baltimore.

The personal factor has almost disappeared in many sales areas. The patient and accommodating salespeople who once counseled and assisted customers at the point of purchase are hard to find. They have been replaced by self-service retailing and a daily flow of direct mail into the home. Even modern packaging, a miracle of technological development, has come under attack. Many regard it as either a threat to the environment or only a cost-cutting convenience to help the manufacturer. Compounding all these negative factors are the constant headlines and broadcasts announcing the latest developments in corporate or government bribery, illegal political contributions, faulty production or misrepresentation of goods, and callous or careless management of employees and natural resources.

In view of such developments and observations, it is no wonder corporate management questions the chances of success of even the best intentioned consumer affairs communications effort.

A Counterbalance that Counts

Any management that sets in motion a consumer affairs communications program must be realistic about the problems of conveying its messages. But that same management should also bear in mind the astonishing public participation in the nationwide celebration that took place on July 4, 1976. The spontaneous and moving celebrations during the bicentennial anniversary reaffirmed the trust of the American people in themselves and the 200 years of their republic. Throughout the nation that day, U.S. citizens demonstrated their belief in their common heritage and in their system of free enterprise and its open opportunities for all.

The message for consumer affairs professionals is that any such effort, simple or complex, can be recognized and approved if it is set on a bedrock of honest conviction. Similarly, a consumer affairs communications program will make its mark if it is solidly placed on a company's desire to tell the truth about what it does and why it does it. Mark Twain long ago set the direction for such enterprise with this piece of advice: "Do what is right. It will please some and astonish the rest."

Although suspicion may be deep rooted in American society, it appears to be balanced by an equally deep rooted desire to trust and believe. Both of these characteristics should be considered in the planning and delivery of a company's consumer affairs activities.

THREE STARTING POINTS

Before developing a successful program, the consumer affairs professional must: (1) understand who and what the public is in our present society; (2) be willing to talk to the public without being condescending; and (3) convince top management that consumer affairs communications is an essential, not peripheral, company concern that requires adequate staff and funding.

Who and What Is the Public?

Until very recently, the publics who make up the aggregate consumer population of the United States were usually identified and compartmentalized by profession or main activities interests—for example, housewife, blue collar worker, teacher, legislator, business or institutional executive, government employee, student, opinion leader, shareholder, or media representative. These identifications are useful in determining the direction and content of consumer and corporate messages.

We are all familiar with the geographical mobility that has become a characteristic of American life. However, another kind of mobility has made the old and rigid classification obsolete. People today are constantly moving in and out of the traditional job or career classifications.

For example, let's briefly examine a day in the life of Margaret A., who is in charge of science studies in a junior high school. Her traditional classification is "teacher." But is this totally appropriate?

Ms. A. arrives at school a few minutes before 8 A.M., having digested her breakfast and listened to the early morning news on the car radio. On the radio, she heard a newscaster say that a drug company in which she owns some stock has announced a breakthrough in the treatment of a form of paralysis. On the same newscast, she heard that three officials of another company, whose product she uses to clean the sink at home, are being charged with embezzling money from the company's employee pension fund. She'll hold her thoughts and opinions about both pieces of news until she can discuss them with other teachers during the morning coffee break.

That day in the classroom, Ms. A. uses a company's instructional pamphlet, prepared specifically for classroom study, on mineral formations. The graphics are good and the text is well suited for her students' age group. Additionally, she has found that the company literature updates some facts in the well-worn textbooks that the school requires her to use for one more year. After her classes are over for the day, Ms. A. becomes a consumer in her local supermarket. Three hours later she takes on another role, that of wife and mother, to serve the evening meal. After the dishes are done, she returns to school, this time as a student in an adult education class. She arrives back home in time to catch the late-evening news. Something that she sees and hears on the screen may cause her to write a letter to her legislative representative about environmental action, gun control, or taxes.

The point of this brief summary of a day in the life of Ms. A. is relatively simple. Although professionally the energetic Ms. A. is a teacher, she may be identified as a member of a number of publics—consumer, wife, parent, student, shareholder, and concerned citizen. In all of these roles, she is a person to be reckoned with. Reaching her with the appropriate corporate message at the right time is more than a corporate challenge; it is a corporate necessity. A successful communications effort must be as diversified as the individuals it hopes to persuade.

Talk To and With—Not Down

All companies must overcome an understandable reluctance to investigate what really goes on in areas where its publics are active, both professionally and after hours.

Schools, for example, are logical dissemination areas for corporate information that has a legitimate and timely link with current programs of study. Frequently, however, these materials are written, designed, and distributed by people who have based their communications program on their own past experience and not on current teaching practices. As a result, millions of dollars' worth of corporate films, brochures, teachers' guides, and instructional aids are distributed but not used.

Some companies take pride in their willingness to "talk business" with employees. Yet a great share of their material is totally inappropriate for the contemporary American employees who handle their own home mortgages, prepare their annual IRS returns, finance college educations for their children, and ask pertinent questions of their brokers before making investment decisions. Companies that use sophisticated research to incorporate subtle nuances of their product advantages in print and broadcast advertising are often satisfied with information techniques in employee communications programs that are far out of date.

A common bit of advice magazine editors give aspiring writers is to "study the book." That means that before writers start a project for a publication, they should carefully study the publication's editorial tone, slant, level of language, and readership profiles. The advice is equally sound for any company trying to communicate its consumer affairs actions to such various audiences as service clubs, stockholders, and opinion leaders. They should know where to place the message, who the readership is, what the best graphics are, and so forth. Just as writers must "study the book," consumer affairs communications specialists must "study the public." Only then are the chances good for the acceptance of the message.

Do You Have the Staff and Funds to Do the Job?

American business is indignant, and often rightly so, at the cost of government regulation. On the other hand, business must also ask itself where it fails in using its own huge communications investment to convince its public of its responsiveness. Part of the problem may be that consumer affairs communications has had a generally low priority in top management's allocation of talent and funds. A company that uses all the communications techniques and expertise to sell products also must use those techniques to sell itself.

CHECKPOINTS FOR ACTION

There are five questions that a public relations manager can use as checkpoints in establishing a consumer affairs communications plan.

1. Have I Checked All the Open Communications Avenues?

The number of communications channels continues to expand along with the volume of communications activity. The invention of cold type has increased the speed of printing. A generation ago, the principal difference in radio stations was their call letters. Today, the radio broadcasting mix in any city is made up of outlets specializing in news, popular music, and classical music. Some have a mix of all three. A few years ago, the function of a T-shirt was to cover the upper torso. Today, lettered T-shirts are often used to good advantage by organizations as diverse as the Metropolitan Opera and General Motors.

Some companies still consider product queries from consumers as a necessary nuisance that can best be handled by a few form letters. More alert companies answer these queries with tact, care, and intelligence. They are aware that an informed consumer can be a willing and persuasive company spokesman for years to come. Long-established service clubs are recognized by many companies as good audiences for speakers' bureaus. Other companies have expanded their bureaus to include such newer audiences as senior citizen groups, special interest constituencies, and adult education classes.

To summarize, effective consumer affairs communications management involves an understanding of the many vehicles available for messages and a willingness to use them.

2. *Do I Recognize that Risks Are Justified?*

The most productive achievements in consumer affairs communications have been undertaken with a full realization of the risk involved. No standard forecasts, for example, could have predicted that a short motion picture shown by the Johnson Wax Company during the 1964–1965 World's Fair would become a major attraction. *To Be Alive,* a sensitive and beautiful film on the possibilities for fulfillment in human existence, carried minimal sponsor identification and no mention of the company's products. Yet this film stole the show at the World's Fair. Years later, it still draws capacity audiences as part of the company's welcome to visitors at its world headquarters in Racine, Wisconsin.

That motion picture is only one of many innovative public affairs programs that Johnson Wax has originated. Its management hired Frank Lloyd Wright to design the dramatic architecture that identifies its headquarters, reflecting the company's pride in its midwestern origin and roots. Johnson Wax has experimented with new housing complexes to prove that affordable living does not have to rest on conventional construction. It has developed new forms of teaching aids for schools, which emphasize the pleasure as well as the essentials of home care and housekeeping. Such actions have helped expand consumer awareness of Johnson as a company that is proud of itself and its product lines and ventures.

Another example of a company's willingness to take a risk in its public information practices is provided by Mobil Oil Corporation. This major petroleum producer and marketer launched a series of company statements several years ago on the Op-Ed page of *The New York Times*. These have run counter to the conventional advertising dictum, "Be brief, be bright, be gone." Mobil's public statements in the *Times*—centered primarily on the need for the petroleum industry to operate without excessive government interference—have been lengthy, literate, and hard hitting. Moreover, they have competed for attention on a newspaper page that probably has the highest level of opinion writing in the country. These statements succeeded in capturing reader respect and attention because of their clear inference that Mobil believes it is acting not only in its own self-interest but in the larger interest of preserving the free enterprise system in which the company has grown and thrived.

3. Is the Information I Offer Accurate and Honest?

Disclosures of falsehood, bribery, illegal or improper lobbying, and reluctant or partial disclosure of executive action in government and business have seriously eroded the faith of Americans in many of their most basic institutions.

The road back is rocky. There are no shortcuts appearing on the skyline. Total honesty in presenting the facts about products, services, or policies is the only course for a company that cares about its reputation and public esteem for its actions. Honesty today enables a company to meet the future by building a reservoir of public understanding that will be available when unexpected problems arise. No business can ever expect to travel blissfully toward a problem-free future. The willingness of a company to be truthful in good times is the best assurance for public understanding and support when the going gets rough.

4. Do I Have the Creative Freedom I Need to Accomplish Our Communications Needs?

It is very doubtful that the Elam's Old Fashioned Buckwheat Mix package will ever win a prize for graphic brilliance or stylish copy. The opening statement on the side panel states that "Elam's was founded in 1917 by Frank Elam. Mr. Elam sold the company in 1944 and has since passed away." The panel copy goes on to make a modest, but completely convincing, claim that good buckwheat flour should be stone ground, that only the whole grain of buckwheat is used by the company, and that "the top of the two-pound size package is resealable if you open it carefully." It ends with the message that "if we can help you in any way, please don't hesitate to write us. We are always happy to hear from you."

Someone at Elam's has creative freedom. The writer has used modest copy to indicate the mood and character of a company that respects its founder, offers a straightforward description of the product, believes that the customer is sufficiently intelligent to reseal the package without involved instruction, and hopes that users might care to write a line or two to say what they think of the flour.

Both Mobil's statements in the *Times* and Elam's packaging are convincing examples of freedom of choice in selecting a communications medium. What is more, the companies say something in that medium that has a good chance of contributing to public understanding and approval.

5. Am I Communicating All the Positive Consumer Advantages that Can Develop Maximum and Positive Public Response?

For some years, one of the nation's major universities has engaged in a vigorous communications program to increase the amount of private gifts and bequests. It uses all the contemporary and sophisticated communications techniques available. One of its least expensive communications actions is the occasional training session for building and grounds personnel to emphasize courtesy in dealing with visitors.

Not long ago, a visitor drove into the university grounds to attend a university function, saw that the parking lots were full, and prepared to turn about and leave the grounds. He was stopped by a guard who said he would do his best to find a spot for the automobile and then did so. A month later, the university received a check in the mail for $3 million. With it came a short note to the effect that a university whose people went out of their way to accommodate a visitor was most likely a good educational investment as well.

That incident shows there is no certain way to determine what part of a consumer affairs communications program will achieve a positive consumer response. The only certain point is that nothing should be overlooked.

The *Queen Elizabeth II* is the fastest liner on the world's oceans. Speed is perhaps the greatest asset the *QE II* possesses over its competition, an advantage that has been merchandised steadily and expertly by the Cunard Line in advertising and publicizing its flagship. But speed is only one part of the appeal of the *QE II*. The main attraction for some is the elegant style of life aboard the ship during a cruise or trans-Atlantic crossing. Others respond to the noble tradition of British seafaring represented by this last and greatest of the Cunard Queens. Still others may have made their decision to sail someday on the *QE II* after attending an open house or special event held on her decks or in her salons. Still others respect her safety record as the point that tips the purchase-of-ticket balance toward Cunard. Different publics, different responses—but all of them valid and all of them based on the communications mix used by the company to present the full range of strengths that are part of the personality of a majestic and accommodating vessel.

○ The action of a parking lot guard in taking the extra bit of trouble.

o Some homespun writing on a package of buckwheat flour.

o A strong statement of company position on the editorial page of one of the country's most respected newspapers.

o A response to a customer's letter that directly and personally speaks to the complaint or problem she is having with a product.

o A T-shirt that says that grand opera is for everybody.

o A news release that spells out why a company is changing its pension plan, channeled to the right media for the publics the company believes will be interested.

All these activities, diverse as they are, indicate the importance of sound consumer affairs communications. Such a program is essential to a company's effort to build confidence among its various publics.

15: Special Projects and Events

WHEN THERE IS a need to create excitement, to capture the imagination, to call attention to something in a way that cannot be ignored, the best approach can often be an event. An event is a publicity device used to draw attention to a product or an organization. Its principal use is to attract media attention to something that is not inherently newsworthy.

A new product that dramatically saves time in all likelihood will be extensively covered in the media. A recent example of a product with high media interest is the home videotape recorder. It frees people from broadcast schedules and is available at a cost within the reach of many consumers. Consequently, the home videotape recorder has received extensive coverage by the media.

The introduction of a new television set with improved tuning features, however, is not likely to interest many writers and broadcasters, because it is only a variation of a well-established product. Faced with the likelihood of being ignored by the media, the manufacturer may choose to stage an event. The manufacturer may decide, for example, to install a television set on every floor of every hospital in a city during the Super Bowl as a way of calling attention to the product.

Organizations and companies also use events to direct attention to their achievements or functions. A manufacturing plant may hold an open house to show off its recently completed modernization program. Charitable groups hold bike-a-thons, auctions, and benefit dinners to raise money and also to increase awareness within the community.

In almost all cases, the main advantage of holding an event is not the number of people who actually attend the event but rather the much greater number who can be reached through the media coverage.

Although an event can be a powerful communications tool, it is also fraught with potential problems. The manager confronted with making the decision about whether or not to authorize an event needs to take a number of factors into consideration.

The overriding consideration is: Will this event successfully communicate my message in the best possible way? Events are essentially "one-shots" and usually require spending a substantial amount of money. This means that the staging of an event must have benefits that cannot be obtained through more traditional means of communication.

Before staging an event, a manager must determine if sufficient human resources are available to make this event work. An event is a very visible attempt to make something happen in a way that will reflect favorably on the organization or product. Nothing is more embarrassing than to conduct an event that falls short of the mark. Events by their nature tend to be complicated. A significant number of people must be available to work on the event, and the project must be directed by a person who is capable of coordinating all the aspects of the event without losing sight of its overall objective.

It is essential to consider how the media will perceive the event. If the event is too blatantly commercial or patently dull, the media will simply not cover it. If the event is less than what was promised and the media do cover it, the risks of highly unfavorable coverage are very great.

Events are excitement vehicles. Managers frequently get caught up in the excitement but fail to examine the event for its ability to meet the communications objectives for the product or the organization. In the case of an event designed to promote a product, a manager must evaluate how easy it will be to cover both the event and the product.

Coverage should communicate the essence of what the product

does and how it should be used. Some events may achieve brand name recognition but contribute nothing to the consumer's knowledge of how or why a product works.

If an event meets the standards established above, the manager will find a number of positive aspects inherent in staging events. For one, because events are exciting, they tend to interest all levels of people both in and outside a company. In the case of a nonprofit organization, an event can be a unifying element, the common task everyone works diligently to make successful. If the event involves a product, it gives the sales force something new and topical to talk to prospects about.

Events have the potential to be different and unique. If you are planning an event for media coverage it must offer something worth covering, something that will interest the media. When an event is covered by the media, it automatically assumes a role of importance and excitement.

Event Ideas

Coming up with an event idea that will attract media attention is a difficult job. Obviously, no one event is suitable for every product or organization at any given time.

The idea must be a skillful blending of product or organization message and an interest-generating happening. Often the event is not directly related to the product or organization; for example, it may be a photographic exhibit, a marathon, or a concert. The interests borrowed from such activities must be strong enough to attract media attention but not so strong or so far afield that they detract from the product or organization.

Take, for example, a photographic exhibit sponsored by a frozen food manufacturer. The objective of the manufacturer was to create a favorable image for its products among working women. The exhibit, which showed working women in both traditional and new work situations, offered the manufacturer a chance to sponsor something that appealed directly to a developing new market. Additionally, the exhibit presented a good opportunity for media to cover a topical subject and at the same time the sponsoring company without compromising the integrity of the media. Any event that makes the media seem to be offering free advertising has little or no chance of media acceptance.

An event idea must be strong enough to break through the competition from all the hard news and features available to the print and broadcast journalist. A standard open house is an example of an event that's not likely to be covered by the media. However, an open house that's tied to the first operating model of a new product, or the forming of the largest piece of steel ever made, or a tour into a previously restricted area, provides an additional incentive for coverage of the event.

Event ideas should also try to provide as much visual action as possible. Television is especially interested in movement. An open house in which the president of the company makes a speech has little media interest. However, if the president pushes a button that pours a ladle of molten steel, television news producers are much more likely to be interested.

Almost all successful events involve action. The Milton Bradley Company, manufacturers of toys and games, was able to use an event to successfully reintroduce its Twister game because the game has so much action.

Twister is a game in which the players stand on a thin plastic sheet covered with six different colored circles. At the direction of a moderator, the players must place their hands and feet on the colored circles without losing their balance. The game usually ends with the competitors' bodies twisted around one another in muscle-straining, odd, and amusing positions.

The event that Milton Bradley selected to promote Twister was held in Fort Lauderdale during the annual spring migration of college students to the Florida beaches. The media obviously liked the concept and execution of the event because of the photographic opportunities with young men and women in a competition of controlled contortion. Wire services used photographs of the event, local television stations covered the event, and there were network feeds for both radio and television.

Managing the Event

All events, regardless of how large or small, need an event manager. This is the person who coordinates all the elements required to execute an event successfully.

The manager will develop the entire blueprint for executing the event after company management has approved the concept. Most event managers use a form similar to a PERT chart that identifies the day for the completion of each step in the plan. These steps may include the rental of special equipment, the contacting and approval of local authorities, all publicity functions surrounding the event, and the hiring of a celebrity to participate. Depending on the size and complexity of the event, the event manager may either work alone or supervise the people responsible for making all the elements happen on time.

A dinner featuring a national celebrity, for example, might only require a single person handling publicity and arrangements. On the other hand, when the Yamaha Motorcycle Division of Nippon Gakki, Inc., staged massive outdoor events to teach people how to ride motorcycles, the event manager coordinated a full-time staff of 28 people and used another 20 people on a part-time basis.

An event manager, regardless of the size of the event, must be detail oriented and budget conscious. He must know every element and its place in making a successful event.

Budgets for events are invariably underestimated. This is particularly true for the contingency section of the budget; budgets for events should always have a contingency section.

The event manager must know the realistic top limits of a budget and the point beyond which there is no more money. This is vital because a curious thing seems to happen to most events and event managers.

Somewhere in the planning of an event it becomes obvious that there are innumerable opportunities for making an event better. This may be by adding more equipment, having more people on the scene, or upgrading materials within the existing program. Because event managers realize that they will be judged by the successful execution of the event—and as the deadline draws closer success always looks more remote—a willingness to do virtually anything that might improve the event develops. This is somewhat insidious because it begins with the event manager making small decisions to upgrade in a number of areas. Almost inevitably, this snowballs into constantly opting for bigger and better elements all along the line.

An experienced event manager recognizes the temptation and resists the urge to spend more. A good event manager always brings new opportunities or obvious flaws in the existing plan to the attention of company management but never unilaterally alters the existing plan.

Site Selection and Timing of Events

The location of an event is almost as important as the event itself. Sometimes site selections are obvious, as for the finals for the Hershey National Track & Field Youth Program. In this case, the finals are held at Charleston, West Virginia, which has the only suitable track and field stadium close to the headquarters of the National Track & Field Hall of Fame. In most cases, however, the site is selected because of the crowds that it can attract and the prestige that it can lend to the event.

The media are generally unimpressed with events that fail to attract a large crowd. A large crowd seems to legitimize the event. *Large* is a relative term, but for events it generally means enough people to provide an atmosphere of enthusiasm.

Whenever possible, events should be structured to use existing crowds. For example, enclosed shopping malls are excellent sites for events because they offer a built-in audience. Additionally, shopping malls are promotion conscious and will help provide materials, supplies, and publicity for events.

Recently, the Brown & Williamson Tobacco Company staged ice sculpturing demonstrations and exhibits in shopping malls to introduce a new brand of menthol cigarettes called Arctic Lights. The demonstrations, which were timed to go on throughout the day, succeeded in attracting thousands of potential consumers of the product.

Another advantage of shopping malls as event sites, especially when the number of people who watch the event is important, is that the shopping mall crowd changes constantly and you have a fresh audience to draw on virtually every hour. In the case of the Arctic Lights ice sculpturing demonstrations and exhibits, this was important because one objective of the program was to give samples of the product to those people who wanted them during the demonstrations.

Another positive feature of shopping malls for staging events is that they are generally landmarks within the cities. The media need no special instructions to reach them, and they know the conditions they're likely to encounter once they arrive.

One negative aspect, however, is that shopping malls are frequently located well out of the downtown area where most newspapers and television stations are headquartered.

As previously mentioned, a site can also lend prestige to an event. To give another cigarette example, British American Tobacco Inc. used a collection of photographs of Britain's Royal Family to help introduce its State Express 555 Brand cigarettes into selected major markets in the United States. The photographs were taken by the Earl of Litchfield, a cousin of Queen Elizabeth II and the only photographer who has access to members of the Royal Family in their private lives.

The exhibit was booked into leading photographic galleries in each of the major cities, and the press was invited to special previews. The quality of the galleries was already well known to the reporters in the cities, so they were predisposed to attend the exhibit because they knew it would not have been accepted by the gallery if it were blatantly commercial. The galleries' prestige also contributed to the tone of the articles written about the exhibit and its sponsor.

Timing of an event is important from at least two aspects. First, an event must be timed to fit the media's convenience. Because many events are of a marginal nature and easily supplanted by a hard news event, it is best to select a time when most media are likely to need news and features. If the principal aim of the event is to attract television coverage, then a weekend day is the best time. Although it is true that television stations have fewer camera crews working on the weekend, it is also true that less local news usually takes place. If your event provides an opportunity for a light news feature, it is even better for television stations that seem to seek news on weekends that is lighter than the news fare during the week.

If your event has a key happening, be sure to inform the television station when that's likely to take place. Nothing irks a television crew more than to have to stand around waiting for something worth filming to occur.

Heinz U.S.A. Division of the H. J. Heinz Company introduced a wine vinegar, used for making salad dressing, into 21 major markets by literally building 300-pound salads in each of the cities. Television crews were alerted to the time that the gigantic salad would be "tossed" by local dignitaries. The visual action of tossing a 300-pound salad was enough to bring television and still photographers, reporters, and broadcasters to this midweek event.

Publicity Surrounding Events

One of the strongest justifications for expending the effort and money required to put on any event is that the event provides numerous opportunities for publicity before and after it takes place. In effect, the event serves as a centerpiece for publicity.

In the case of its wine vinegar introduction, Heinz was able to spin off a number of activities to get media attention. These included arranging for the mayors of all the cities to declare "Salad Week"; sending a home economist into the city to do radio, television, and newspaper interviews announcing the gigantic salad; providing home economics classes in each city with a one-period lesson plan for learning about salads; following up the gigantic salads by sending a series of salad recipes, all using Heinz wine vinegar, to weekly and daily newspapers and tying in the recipes with advertising.

TreeSweet brand orange juice used the distribution of coupons by high school students as the preliminary to an event. TreeSweet contributed money to high school athletic funds on the basis of the number of coupons redeemed. This effort was the centerpiece for publicity involving a personal appearance by TreeSweet's spokesman O. J. Simpson. In each market, O. J. participated in a press conference and a photo-taking session involving the student leaders from each of the high schools participating in the program. Those photos were subsequently distributed to weekly newspapers in the students' neighborhoods, and a news clip concerning the TreeSweet program was sent to local television stations.

In connection with Milton Bradley's National Team Twister Contest, news releases generated by the contest and photographs of participants were used to generate publicity in hometown media. In addition, a booklet called "Twister Contests for Fun and Fund-Raising" was produced to explain how to use a Twister competition as a charitable money-raising activity.

As part of the Arctic Lights ice sculpturing exhibit, the ice sculpturers were interviewed for television, radio, and newspaper before the event, and a booklet on ice sculpturing and ice molds for home entertaining was offered to those who viewed the sculpturing.

A good publicist should be able to program several pre- and postevent activities to maximize publicity from any event.

Use of Celebrities

We live in an age of celebrities. The media continue to be fascinated by these people who have gained fame in sports, show business, and politics. If a celebrity is pertinent to an event, the event can benefit from his or her involvement.

Generally, a celebrity is useful because the media know that even if nothing else happens at the event they can at least interview the celebrity and get a story.

However, the greatest danger in using celebrities is that the media may interview them about their activities rather than about the event and the product or organization it is designed to promote. When Hi-C Drinks, a product of the Coca-Cola Foods Division, used Lynn Swann, the all-pro wide receiver for the Pittsburgh Steelers, as its spokesman for a series of Frisbee Disc competitions, Swann had to be carefully trained to redirect questions that concerned the Super Bowl and violence in professional football to his own relationship to the Hi-C-sponsored program.

A celebrity must be both capable and willing to turn the conversation to the sponsoring organization. A celebrity should be hired only after he clearly understands the role he will play in the event and states his willingness to promote the sponsoring organization.

Testing an Event

Many events are developed to be modular units that can be staged in a number of markets with essentially the same format in each. In these market-by-market events, the goal is generally to achieve not national publicity but major publicity within each market. Market testing is an important factor in modular events designed for multimarket use.

An event is tested usually for two purposes. First, to determine the receptivity of the media to the idea and the type of coverage the event will generate. Second, to determine logistical difficulties inherent in staging the event.

The Heinz wine vinegar giant salad program was tested in four markets before the company approved implementation in 17 other markets. Among other things, Heinz tested staging the event in an outdoor location at a shopping center, at a hockey game, and in an enclosed shopping mall. Malls were ultimately chosen because of their efficiency and the built-in crowds. The tests also helped smooth the procedures for working with the local health departments, which had to approve the making of a large salad that was to be consumed by the public.

In addition, Heinz learned how to handle questions from the media about the salads and their preparation. The company also found out the best way to dispose of the leftover food after the event (it was generally donated to the local zoo) and the best timing for these events so they would coincide with consumer purchase opportunities.

Testing is especially important for an event where a crowd is not readily available but must be generated. In Yamaha's Learn-To-Ride program, a crowd of people had to be attracted to a specific area. Yamaha tested its promotion procedures and learned that it could obtain local police and highway safety department approval for its event. It also discovered that special media-only Learn-To-Ride events helped contribute to drawing a crowd and to overall participation.

The actual running of a multimarket event will usually cost somewhat less than the test run. In testing the event, an organization may wish to produce an inexpensive version of the literature to be distributed to the people who attend. Celebrities, on the other hand, will usually request more money for a single appearance than they could for each appearance as part of a multiple-appearance contract.

It is not uncommon for the cost of a test run to be twice as much as per market costs in a multimarket rollout of the event.

Some Common Observations about Events

People who have conducted a large number of events have made some basic observations that apply to almost all situations:

○ Don't expect regional field salespeople to be much help in staging an event. They generally have plenty to do already and cannot become involved other than to suggest local suppliers of materials.

○ Events with local tie-ins always seem to work best. Incorporating local celebrities and charities makes the event seem designed especially for that market and invariably elicits more cooperation from the media.

○ No matter how cooperative the management is at a local site, it will be too busy to help much during the actual event.

○ Always try to put together the event materials in a self-contained package. Don't count on others to supply loudspeakers, electric cords, stanchions, and the like.

○ Always cordon off the event area. Crowds are curious and likely to want to touch any equipment or materials that are used.

○ Never conceal the sponsoring organization or the real reason for running an event from the media. Any deception will become obvious once reporters and broadcasters attend, and they're likely to feel duped and treat the event negatively.

○ A successful event should be fun for the participants as well as the crowd.

○ All equipment rented from local suppliers should be delivered before the day of the event. It is better to pay for two days of equipment rental than it is to try to track down a supplier on the day of the event.

○ Always prepare remarks for celebrities to use at the event. Many celebrities are poor ad-libbers and will disappoint the audience with their stumbling and lack of poise.

○ It is difficult to hold the attention of a shopping mall crowd for more than a half hour. Time the key elements of your event to last no longer than that.

Events have become increasingly popular in recent years for several reasons. The nature and length of local television news has made well-structured events especially useful to the medium. Also, events provide an opportunity for maximum market coverage in a single day.

Events are totally involving opportunities that are very visible. Whereas many publicity efforts are done behind the scenes, an event is a direct bid for media coverage. The risk is greater in using an event to seek publicity but so are the rewards.

16: Corporate Advertising

CORPORATE ADVERTISING and public relations are often closely allied. Both deal with the image of a corporation as expressed through its public communications, and both attempt to shape public attitudes. The main difference between them is that corporate advertising, unlike public relations, can select the exact content of the message as well as the media in which it will appear.

Many corporations have chosen to supplement their traditional public relations activities with paid communications. What advertising may lack in credibility, especially on controversial issues, it makes up for in its ability to organize the communications strategy and to plan it thoroughly.

If control of the information, the amount of coverage, and timing are especially important to a client, it is recommended that they consider corporate advertising. If the subject is highly specialized or closely linked with a current public relations project, such as a stock tender offer, the PR professional may be used to prepare the advertising. In this way the client is able to have the best talent available for a particular project, without taking extra time or spending more money to educate new writers. For a substantial or a particularly complex program, however, it is wise to seek counsel from someone experienced in the special skills of corporate advertising.

The link between public relations and corporate advertising also carries over to the client side. Corporate advertising managers are more likely to have a public relations background than to have come to the job through the marketing department. In smaller companies, or those that seldom use corporate advertising (such as food or drug companies), the public relations director normally handles the function.

An increasing number of companies have unified communications departments that supply both public relations and corporate advertising services. These departments are known variously as corporate communications, public affairs, or simply advertising and public relations. In general the department reports directly to top corporate management. According to the Association of National Advertisers, only about 5 percent of their members do in-house creative work for corporate advertising; most use the same agencies that handle their product advertising.

Another characteristic that PR and corporate advertising practitioners must both contend with is the difficulty of proving their worth. The test of an effective PR program is not the quantity of printer's ink used or the number of chairs filled; it is the amount of opinion that is controlled, the attitudes that are changed, or the impressions that are left with the public. In the same way, corporate advertising does not enjoy the luxury of being able to relate the amount of promotion to the number of responses to a direct sales message.

Accountability should be the watchword for all comprehensive communications programs. Research that measures the changes in awareness, understanding, and attitudes about the company is particularly important to justify such substantial expenditures. If you are the champion of the corporate image, you must challenge your department and your agency to document at every turn the effectiveness of corporate advertising.

DEFINITIONS

Defining corporate advertising is like trying to nail pudding to the wall. One is forced into vague generalities such as "advertising designed to portray a desirable corporate image," or negative statements such as "advertising that is not meant to sell a product," or hyperbole such as "advertising that sells the company." Corporate advertising is also called general promotion or institutional, image, issue, strategic, or umbrella advertising. The labels are often more confusing than helpful.

Perhaps the most accurate way to define corporate advertising is to consider the obvious. Quite simply, it is advertising authorized at the corporate level. This statement can give us greater insight than many simplistic definitions and buzz words. It says that corporate advertising must:

Have the commitment of top management.

Be for the general good of the enterprise, since it is management's function to protect the stockholder's investment.

Complement the corporate plan for continued growth and not be at odds with the product advertising programs.

Be considered more as a capital expenditure than as a short-term business expense.

Be given sufficient time and continuity to prove its effectiveness.

Have as much substantiation as other multimillion-dollar corporate projects if it is to last.

Corporate advertising is the voice of management. It helps shape a corporate image. It is more concerned with "who" is advertising than with "what" is being advertised. It creates goodwill and confidence toward the total company rather than directing attention to any particular product. If an advertisement features a product, it is meant to represent the capabilities, resources, know-how, or even conscience of the company.

Although the purposes of product and corporate advertising may differ, the structure of the communications plan should be similar. Each should identify the current situation by an internal analysis of strengths and weaknesses. Each should determine immediate objectives and long-term goals, whether it is share of market or share of mind. And each should formulate a strategy, implement it, and measure the results.

OBJECTIVES

A 1979 survey of current practices in the use of corporate advertising among members of the Association of National Advertisers (ANA) showed the following ranking of primary objectives:

1. To improve the level of awareness of the company, the nature of its business interests, and its profitability.
2. To provide unified marketing support for the company's present and future products, services, or capabilities.
3. To enhance or maintain the company's reputation and goodwill.
4. To inform or educate about subjects of importance to the company's future (such as economics, resource allocations, or government policies).
5. To advocate (or oppose) specific actions on issues of importance to the company, its industry, or business in general.
6. To communicate the company's concern and record of achievement on social or environmental issues.

Since the ANA survey is repeated every two years, it is interesting to track changes in priority. For example, the top two objectives—awareness improvement and unified marketing support—have risen considerably since 1975. Both are encouraging trends: the former, because its goals can be expressed in measurable terms; the latter, because it reflects a newfound appreciation that good corporate advertising can affect the bottom line.

The third objective about reputation and goodwill was ranked first in the 1975 survey. But, since it is so vague, few should mourn its fall. The fourth objective needs to be treated very carefully since it contains the potential for one of the fatal flaws of corporate advertising—assuming that subjects of importance to the company's future are necessarily of interest to your audience. It is also curious that the lowest-priority objectives that deal with "advocacy" or "issue" advertising are generally the ones that have been given the most press coverage. It would seem that much of the debate about the freedom of commercial speech is a false, or at least a narrow, controversy.

There can be many other compelling reasons to use corporate advertising. An obvious one is a change in the corporate name. Such advertising is needed to protect the enormous investment made by a company during years of building a reputation for its products and services. Another reason might be that a company's image has not kept up with its activities, so that image and reality are out of phase. Key publics may still identify the company with whole product lines that have been changed, discontinued, or divested. Or the company may have made acquisitions that need to be explained to clarify the corporation's future goals.

Corporate advertising may also be used to pave the way for companies that are contemplating changes in their long-term strategies and business plans. Such preparations will help customers, employees, investors, suppliers, and even government regulators accept such changes. Often a company can extend its established reputation for product quality in one area to lesser-known product lines. Corporate advertising can make possible the transfer of such positive attributes as reliability, technological capabilities, and responsiveness to customer needs.

Recruitment and employee relations are common secondary objectives for corporate advertising. A company's future depends on attracting and keeping good people on the job. Companies spend thousands of dollars training each skilled worker and executive. The recognition gained from certain kinds of corporate advertising can protect and sustain this valuable resource.

Healthy community relations can also be maintained by the judicious use of corporate advertising in plant or headquarters cities. There undoubtedly are many other logical uses for corporate advertising. Carefully thought-out programs, made accountable to measurable objectives, can be used to balance various potential risks to the corporation.

STRATEGIES

Sound marketing and advertising plans begin with a strategic analysis of the current situation. Corporate advertising is no exception. To attain an objective, you must first understand where you are, where you think you should be, and the resources you will need to get there. A company contemplating corporate advertising intended to create, maintain, or restore a favorable image must start by evaluating how it is perceived by the key publics that will have the greatest influence on the corporation's future. Here are some basic questions that must be answered before an effective corporate advertising strategy can be developed.

1. What is the self-image of the corporation? What are its strengths, and what makes it unique?
2. What are the company's long-term business goals?
3. How well known is the company? How does the company's recognition compare with that of the competition?
4. How is your company influenced by attitudes toward particular industries and toward business in general? Are you bucking any major social changes?
5. How do people currently get information about the company? Is this information reliable, and does it reinforce the proper image?
6. Which are the key target audiences that affect the corporation?
7. How are you perceived by each of these key publics?
8. What are the discrepancies between the desired company position and the actual perception of its position?
9. How important are these differences, and are they likely to be influenced by advertising?
10. Are there different messages for different publics? Will this affect the selection of media?
11. How can the answers to the above questions be translated into measurable goals?

Once this initial evaluation is complete, realistic objectives can be set and budgets established to fulfill the task. It will also serve as a standard for judging the effectiveness of the communications program and the timeliness of the strategy.

TARGET AUDIENCES

Just as the communications strategy must be designed specifically for individual corporate needs, the particular mix of target audiences will vary widely among companies. During 1979, a survey by the ANA (cited earlier) found that its members set multiple purposes for their corporate advertising:

	Primary Target (%)	Secondary Target (%)	Combined Total (%)
Business community	39	31	70
Financial community	27	34	61
Government and related	9	29	38
Employees/plant communities	6	31	37
Activists/opinion leaders	13	21	34
The entire adult public	17	10	27
Specific segments of the public (such as regional audiences, those with upscale income or education, and those of a particular sex or race)	25	5	30

Generally speaking, smaller advertisers are more interested in reaching stockholders, trade associates, and the financial community. Larger advertisers are inclined to add the general public, opinion leaders, and government officials. Consumer goods companies are interested in government officials and the general public. Industrial companies are more concerned about the financial community.

MEDIA SELECTION

To reach their target audiences, the ANA members used the following media for their corporate messages:

Business magazines	71%	General newspapers	19%
Specialized newspapers	53	Local radio	17
General magazines	43	Direct mail	16
National television	36	Public television	12
Local television	23	National radio	5

Because of relative costs, the distribution of budgets would be different from the one shown here. More than half of all corporate advertising spending is now in television, since the larger advertisers are more apt to include the general public in their audience mix.

Media should be selected to carry advertising on the basis of their efficiency in reaching the target audiences. Other criteria include the size of the budget, reach and frequency goals, geographical considerations, the appropriate season, editorial atmosphere, and the complexity of the message. The basic principles of media planning are similar for corporate and product advertising. There is a difference, however, in the background of the people who make the final decisions and their level in the organization.

Clients should be involved in the media selection process at the highest possible corporate level. The decisionmakers on a corporate advertising account often have strong opinions about different media. It helps to know these in advance to save time and effort, so that counterarguments can be presented or options adjusted.

The client should be prepared to help his agency by supplying priorities for different target audiences. For example, if business managers are your prime target audience, how important is it to reach private investors? In this way, weights can be assigned to each target audience in the company's combination of key publics. A system like this is both understandable to corporate management and useful for agency media planning purposes.

It is now possible to use the computer and syndicated media research to sort through a number of choices among print and broadcast vehicles. When the selection process is applied to a particular mix of weighted target audiences, a "benchmark" media plan is generated. This optimum plan can then be compared with alternative media plans. The client will know exactly what is being sacrificed in target-audience reach and in message frequency. Perhaps a better editorial fit with the advertising message will tip the scale to the alternative plan, but it will be part of a rational selection process.

MEASURING EFFECTIVENESS

Since there are so many things that can affect a company's public image, it is very difficult to isolate the effect of corporate advertising alone. However, this should not deter you from taking every opportunity to test public perceptions of the corporation, its products, and its services. There are many case histories of successful corporate advertising, but since every company's situation is different, they cannot replace primary research.

Eighty-four percent of the ANA members who use corporate advertising conduct periodic attitude-tracking studies. Thirty percent use research to establish advertising objectives. Twelve percent use research to establish spending levels.

Secondary methods of tracking corporate advertising effectiveness include requests for a response device such as the annual report, letters from the public, the opinions of company officials, feedback from employees, and comments in the media. It is less common to expect bottom-line results such as sales or stock price increases.

Several ambitious studies have attempted to substantiate the effectiveness of corporate advertising in general. Their method is to compare companies that use corporate advertising with those that do not, or that use it only sparingly. In one such study conducted by Yankelovich Skelly and White for *Time* in 1979, it was found that corporate advertisers outscored nonadvertisers in every area studied (recall, +42%; familiarity, +48%; overall impression, +30%; and potential supportive behavior, +33%), regardless of product advertising expenditures, sales revenue, or P/E ratios. Other studies have found a positive, statistically significant effect on stock prices.

CONCLUSION

It is estimated that annual corporate advertising expenditures are now close to $500 million. Furthermore, the category is expected to grow at a rate of 20 percent a year for the next five years. Such an enormous investment deserves sufficient planning, analysis, and documentation. In many ways corporate advertising is more complex than other communications methods, yet it has often been treated in the least systematic manner.

Attention to corporate advertising by professional communicators has also been growing, however. Those in the field are looking eagerly for ways to improve the effectiveness of their messages and of the media selection process. Corporate advertising is on its way to becoming a more precise communications tool.

17: Corporate Identity and Graphics

ONE ONLY HAS TO LEAF through the Yellow Pages to see that very few companies of any size do not have an identifying logotype. A logo has become as much an integral part of most business enterprises as income tax forms. You can rest assured that the selection of the logo was made by top management, in many cases by the chief executive officer. But logos, unlike chief executive officers, live on and on and are changed with great reluctance—unless, of course, they are simply something that looks good on letterheads.

But sometimes logos have to be changed. It may be that the CEO is uncomfortable with the existing one, but more likely the logo has become obviously outdated. This may be because the company has expanded into new product lines, become a conglomerate, or found that the logo does not accurately portray the real function of the company. The corporate communications manager may suggest new logos and graphics, or he may be directed to implement their creation.

It's very easy to have someone do a logo for you. It is the kind of assignment that artists love, because it draws on their creative talents and is something they can point to for years as an accomplishment. A logo, if it is used extensively by a large company, may very well be the most visible artwork that an artist will ever do.

But before approaching an artist, the corporate manager should understand what a logo is intended to do. If he is the one who is suggesting that a new logo be developed, then he should have some solid reasons to back up that proposal.

A graphic designer can probably tell if a logo is working for the company, but he may have difficulty articulating that in terms the chief executive officer will accept. You'll need something more solid than the artist's evaluation. We recommend that you conduct a survey to determine the impact of the existing logo on various segments of the public. From that, you will be able to find out if in fact the logo is widely recognized and if it projects the image the company desires. Some logos seem old fashioned, but that is not all bad if the company has a product that may best be marketed as having the quality of the "good old days." But principally, most companies want to be perceived as modern, efficient, progressive, expanding, and so forth. A survey will help to gauge whether the existing logo accomplishes your objectives.

The importance of a logo and graphics must be placed in perspective. A good logo won't make a company successful any more than the color of a jockey's silks will make a lame horse run faster. And a bad logo won't make a company a failure. However, all things being equal, a good logo can help your business. Many consider logos to be cosmetic, and there's a lot of truth in that. You are far more likely to go into a store that has an attractive front than one that looks mundane or seedy. The products in both stores may be the same. In fact, those in the store with the ordinary front may be better, but you may not go into it to find out. If you are selling second-hand clothing, however, you don't want a storefront that looks as if it is a branch of Nieman-Marcus. That will scare off the customers you are seeking. Remember, a logo is really a sales tool. Even if you are a charitable organization, you want to sell your image to the public. A logo must fit the company or organization for which it is designed. For a company that is going into business, a logo can help build the image that you wish to communicate to the public. The operative word is *help.* Quality service and products are still the backbone of success.

If you initiate the development of a new logo, it is not wise to attack the old one. If you do and it was designed by the chairman's daughter, the chairman may become defensive. That may be an unlikely example, but it is far better to argue the demise of an existing logo with logic than with venom. A survey, of course, is the most useful tool, but in lieu of that, a rational critique of an old logo is the recommended procedure.

If the decision is made to go forward with a new logo and new graphics, only two things are needed to get the work under way: a telephone call and money.

There are several large companies that specialize in the design of logos and graphics. Their portfolios will show that they have been very successful, and you can expect to get a thorough job. You also can expect to pay a substantial amount for the assignment—and if you have the budget, this is probably the safest way to go. In doing so, however, you must have a commitment from management that it is genuinely determined to use the logo and graphics in a way to justify the costs. That includes, in addition to such obvious ways as for stationery and advertising, the use on signs identifying plants and offices, on vehicles and decals, and so forth.

If you are not a large company and don't think the large outlay of money to hire an agency that specializes in graphics is justified, it is possible to find many competent graphic designers who do creditable work for much less of an investment. Your advertising or public relations agency can probably recommend someone to do the job. It's true that many commercial artists may be capable of developing a logo and graphics for you, but you're better off finding someone who is experienced—and successful—in the field.

Some designers will require a flat fee. If that's the case, then it is sure to be substantial enough to cover some false starts in the event the first designs aren't acceptable. Other designers will work on a graduated scale, charging so much for each part of the graphics program.

Whether you hire a specialized agency or a good graphic designer, the procedures they follow will probably be very similar. You should be prepared to help them and also understand what they conceive as the elements of good logos and graphics.

One of the first requests by the graphic designer will be to talk to your top management. The designer will want to find out the realistic goals and aspirations of the company. This is important in the design because, as indicated earlier, logos may have to last for a long time. The designer also will seek to evaluate the existing logo and analyze its shortcomings.

A logo may turn out to be too specific. For example, a Texas company that was involved exclusively in marine products decided on a logo that included a trident. That was fine until the company bought some coal mines. Then it was back to the drawing board.

Designers will tell you that the principal element in a logo is the symbolism. It should create a visual impression that is unconscious and instantaneous—either you see something immediately or you hesitate because you are not quite sure. A logo that confuses the viewer and causes him to ponder about it probably isn't doing the job. Often cliches are used in logos. A company, for example, may want to show that it is moving upward and try to indicate this with arrows or bolts of lightning. In all probability, the interpretation by the viewer will be entirely different from what was intended.

Another major consideration in logo design is flexibility; that is, can it be adapted to a number of different applications? For example, a logo might need to be stamped on the end of a piece of lumber. If it has a number of fine lines, that use may not be feasible. Or it might have to be 20 to 30 feet high to be placed on a hangar door. Or it might need to be used on an arm patch.

Many companies may opt to have their name worked into some kind of symbol. That's possible if the name is short, such as Itex, but if it's Mergenthaler, forget it. The lettering, under any circumstances, should be simple. Any attempt to get tricky may destroy the legibility. Sometimes, a name is enclosed in a shape. This can be difficult to work with because it will inhibit the ability to reduce the logo in size.

Probably, the most common desire of a company in designing a logo is to use its initials. This can work, but only if the company's initials are part of the name it goes by. For example, Pittsburgh Plate Glass Company is now PPG Industries. However, if you are the Allied Beadwork Company, you will hardly get mileage out of ABC. Unless the company is really known by its initials, such as the

American Broadcasting Company, the initials will be no more noteworthy than a shirt monogram.

In working with the graphic designer, make sure to establish deadlines—realistic ones, of course. And make sure he has a firm grasp of what direction you think he should take.

If the gatekeeper—the one who will ultimately say "go" or "no go"—has some very strong convictions about what he wants, then it is folly, unless you are extremely persuasive, to authorize something that is counter to that conviction. Neither the PR director nor the graphic designer should throw in the towel if the gatekeeper's desires are obviously unworkable. It will be both your roles to attempt to lead the discussions to a good solution. That will require the utmost diplomacy. If your reasons are sound, they should be able to carry the day. CEOs didn't get to their positions by being inflexible.

How the graphic designer develops the logo is, of course, his concern, not yours. He undoubtedly will come up with a number of sketches. He'll muse over them, contemplate them, refine them, and ultimately pick a favorite.

At this point, if you are in charge of the project, he may meet with you to get a preliminary judgment on his selection. In all likelihood, if he's been through the mill before, he'll show you only one design. He knows that if he offers three or four, the process of choosing "the right one" becomes very difficult.

If you don't like the one that he's selected, then he's likely to reach in his case and pull out some alternatives. He may not give up on his favorite and tell you why it is superior to the others. If he's from a large design firm, he's probably gone through this exercise with the management. He and the account executive may not throw in the towel easily—after all, large design firms didn't get large by supplying clients with graphics that represent the lowest possible denominator. Their arguments may weaken your resolve, and you may be convinced that they are right. On the other hand, you may have strong ideas too and be unbudged. If that happens, they'll probably ask you to select one of the alternatives. If you do, and they're satisfied you're in the ball park, then you can move on to the next step. If you don't, then they'll grind their teeth, mutter to themselves, and try again.

As corporate communications manager, you should have an important role in the selection. You should have a feel for what the company's top management wants and needs. You may wish to move the selected logo through some other management echelons, but do so with great caution. You should let others know what you are doing—that's good communications. But seeking approval from a number of people may lead you into a morass that may be difficult to extricate yourself from. As you undoubtedly know, there are people who, when you ask for their approval, feel an obligation to make suggestions. And if you don't follow their suggestions, they feel ignored. So keep the number with direct involvement as small as feasible. When you reach a reasonable degree of agreement then the next move is a full-fledged presentation to the top management. That may be the CEO and other senior officers, or it may be the entire board of directors. The presentation should show the logo and graphics in various applications—on signs, invoices, memos, internal and external publications, advertising, and signage.

New logos and graphics are usually introduced in stages; you should have a carefully plotted plan for making the substitution. The obvious things, such as stationery, are usually first. Sometimes it is necessary to destroy slow-moving materials. That may break the accounting department's heart, but you can't wait too long to phase in the new logo.

The principal effort in a corporate identity program will be the development of a logo. It is by far the most important element, because once you have selected it, the logo will set the tone and style for all other graphics the company uses.

Great care should be exercised in selecting the logo; you may have to live with it for a long time. Changing it can be a massive and expensive effort. You will have to place a great deal of faith in the capabilities of the agency or person who will do the job for you. It's wise to depend on expert judgment—but not completely.

18: The Use of Public Relations Counseling

IN THE EARLY DAYS of public relations counseling, a company manager was likely to invite a counselor to tell the company what services the counselor could offer. This is rarely the case today. Now, many corporate managers use a far more precise method in deciding to retain public relations counsel.

This is evident in a 1979 survey of corporate public relations officers, done by Research Strategies Corporation of New York City for Marshall C. Lewis, director of corporate communications for Union Carbide Corporation. Lewis reported the results to a meeting of the Public Relations Counselors Section of the Public Relations Society of America.

The public relations executives in 30 of the largest companies in the United States were asked to evaluate the competence of public relations counselors and the quality of the services they render. Lewis said that the survey, because it involved so many large companies, could be regarded as an unusually representative view of how public relations counselors are perceived by such companies. Seventy-seven percent of those participating were using public relations counsel at the time of the survey.

When the executives were asked to rate the competence of counselors by function—on the basis of either personal experience or simply what they believed to be true—here is how the functions were ranked:

1. Marketing and promotional publicity
2. Third-party objectivity and counsel
3. Early warning system on emerging problems

4. Counseling and planning for issues management and constituency communications
5. Providing government relations support and contact at federal and state levels
6. Corporate publicity and media relations
7. Writing advocacy or "issue" advertising
8. Writing executive speeches, opinion pieces, and by-lined articles
9. Executing state-level campaigns to deal with referenda or ballot issues
10. Handling the writing and execution of constituency communications programs
11. Employee communications—concepts and execution

This is obviously not a complete list of activities that a public relations counselor can perform, but it does provide a checklist for a public relations manager to use in considering outside counsel.

If the decision is to look at agencies, the most useful document is O'Dwyer's *Directory of Public Relations Firms* (published annually by J. R. O'Dwyer Co., Inc., 271 Madison Avenue, New York, N.Y. 10016.) It lists more than 900 public relations firms and public relations departments of advertising agencies and has an index of firms by skill in 14 areas of specialization, including beauty and fashions, financial and investor relations, foods and beverages, home furnishings, and travel. The directory also provides a list of clients of these agencies.

Public relations agencies come in all sizes. Some are specialized. Some provide a variety of services. They can be used effectively, or they can merely be a costly part of the public relations budget.

The largest public relations agency has an annual income of nearly $30 million and employs more than 700 people. Generally, these large agencies have offices in the United States and in many foreign nations. The bulk of public relations agencies, however, have fewer than 10 employees and income of less than $1 million annually.

As might be expected, the larger agencies offer services in diverse geographic settings and are willing to assist in many areas of specialization, such as investor relations, government affairs, employee communications, community relations, consumer publicity, and educational relations. The smaller agencies are of two types: those that handle only one of the special fields of public relations and those that handle any of the areas of public relations, but limit their services to companies and organizations located near their offices.

In deciding which type of agency is best for a particular company, the manager must first analyze the kind of help he will be seeking from the agency. Does he need good advice about what can be done and what cannot be done? If so, he should seek an agency where he will have the attention of senior management with experience in the areas of public relations of concern to his company. The type of service needed might be pure counseling. The agency would assist the manager in researching the public relations problems and identifying the publics to be reached, suggest ways of reaching these publics, and later help evaluate the work performed by the internal public relations department and determine whether the desired results have been achieved.

In order to obtain this type of service, the public relations manager should choose an agency whose senior management is the type that he can deal with regularly and that will be available to him when needed. Size will be of less concern. The most important factor will be the experience of the people in the agency.

If the public relations manager thinks that his staff is too small or too inexperienced to handle a particular function, for instance, investor relations, the search for help will turn in another direction. The manager will then have to decide if his company needs help in many service areas and whether help is needed in preparing presentations to analysts and registered representatives of brokerage firms. The agencies the manager selects for review should have a demonstrated ability to achieve results in investor relations for a corporation of the same size as his own company.

If a public relations manager has a small company staff, the search may be for an agency with personnel who can assist in the actual execution of the communications tasks that are generally involved in a public relations program.

In summary, a decision should be made based on the size of the agency, the special expertise that is needed, and the geographic area of service. The manager must then determine a means of soliciting agencies for review and also construct a rating system to evaluate those agencies that respond.

It is reasonable to assume that the manager will be able to roughly estimate the amount of money he expects to spend on outside services, including out-of-pocket expenses. This information should be supplied to the agencies so they can judge the importance of the potential client and the amount of agency resources to be devoted to the client if the agency gets the assignment. Specific spending levels should be determined only after the agency has outlined a program.

The letter of invitation is usually addressed to the agency's chief executive officer. A questionnaire should be enclosed. This will help to screen out those agencies that have obvious weaknesses or potential client conflicts.

Here are some typical questions to be included in the questionnaire:

Factual Information about the Agency

o How long has the agency been in business?
o What is the total number of people employed by the company?
o Is the agency affiliated with any national agency, organization, or network? How can these organizations serve my company?
o Does the agency specialize in any type of public relations, for example, financial, consumer, association, travel, or industrial?
o Does a single account represent more than 25 percent of the agency's billing or time?
o What was the total billing for each of the last three years and an estimate of the billings for the current year?

○ What accounts have been added and what accounts have been lost in the calendar year prior to the date of the letter?

○ What experience does the agency have that would be of value in its work if it is named as public relations counsel?

Personnel

○ How is the agency organized? (Include an organization chart.)

○ Who are the senior general management and department management executives?

○ Briefly, what is the background of top management, including length of service with the agency and other agencies and client organizations?

○ Who would be assigned to the account and to what extent would these key executives work on the account? Who would have overall responsibility?

Financial Information and Compensation Arrangements

○ What does the agency charge, and does it work on a fee basis?

○ Does the agency have a history of sound profitability?

○ Does the agency prefer compensation by fee or some other methods?

Support Functions

○ Describe the agency's editorial feature story and media placement work.

○ Describe the agency's creative, promotional, merchandising, and research capabilities.

○ Describe the agency's background in the identification of issues and their management.

Agency Business Strategy

○ What is the agency's personality?

○ What are the objectives of the agency as a business enterprise?

o What business strategy has the agency adopted for achieving these objectives?
o How does the agency begin a new client relationship?
o What factors are involved in a sound client–agency relationship?
o What role does the agency envision it will have in developing corporate and marketing plans?
o What are the agency's procedures for insuring consistent flow of information between the agency and the client?

Public Relations Philosophy and Practice

o What do you consider the principal public relations product the agency sells? What is the main competitive advantage it has over other public relations agencies?
o What method is used for controlling the quality of your agency's service, particularly in the area of editorial services and media placement and creative development and execution?
o Submit a brief and concise statement of the agency's public relations philosophy and what it thinks makes public relations effective, what methods are used for developing effective public relations, and how their effectiveness is measured.
o What do you consider the agency's most outstanding public relations achievements in recent years? When did they take place, and why are they considered outstanding?

SUMMARY

o Supply additional reasons that might convince us to hire your agency.
o List some references among the agency's clients.

The answers will give you a good idea of which agencies talk your kind of language and how you relate to them.

The next step is to meet with the agencies that make your cut. It is preferable to have these meetings in two steps. First, invite the agencies to talk at your office. Let them get a feel for you. Second, ask them to make brief capabilities presentations at their offices so you can see how they live and work.

At this point in the agency selection process, some clients provide background on a specific problem and ask the agency to develop an approach but not a complete plan. Some agencies do not like to do this without being paid. Clients now frequently see this step as worthy of compensation to help defray agency costs involved in developing an approach. The amount paid depends on the complexity of the problem. A reasonable payment would be an estimated one month's fee.

Should the manager decide to pursue this method of final selection, it may be wise to ask that the proposed account team make the presentation. Sometimes senior agency management will not work on the account regularly, so this is a way to see how the account team might perform if they are hired.

No program of any sort can be properly prepared unless the objectives and estimated budget for the program are given to the agency.

Here is a checklist of things to consider in evaluating an agency.

I. Internal Performance
   A. Working knowledge of
      The public relations business
      Public relations planning
      Public relations research
      Public relations evaluation
      Marketing and public relations
      Legal aspects of public relations
      Sales promotion
      Production—print and broadcast
      Industry, economics, and social trends as they fit
         client structure
   B. Specific performance
      Overall planning and implementation judgment
      Quality of client contacts and reporting

Frequency of client contacts and reporting
Preparation of client billing and income forecasts
  for internal agency use
Writing skills
Presentation skills
Ability to organize and direct meetings
New business development
New business presentation skills
Overall creative ability in the following areas:
    News and feature writing—print and broadcast
    Speech writing
    Booklets and other printed materials
    Audiovisual presentations
    Programming
    Media placement—print and broadcast
Ability to have productive relationships in client areas with:
    National media
    Local media
Degree of understanding in the following areas:
    Financial communications
    Employee relations
    Community relations
    Product publicity
    Government relations
    Press relations
    Consumer relations
II. Client Performance
  A. Depth of knowledge of
    Client products service
    Client marketing process
    Client competition
  B. Ability to secure client approval on work and budgets
  C. Acceptance at top client levels
  D. Acceptance at middle client levels
  E. Ability to keep client informed of public relations work

F. Ability to demonstrate public relations success to client
G. Acceptance among client's public relations group.

A point rating system can be developed. You should rate the function as to its importance and also how the agency has performed the function as demonstrated in the presentation, in conversations, and in written material:

IMPORTANCE RATING

	Points
Critically important	5
Extremely important	4
Very important	3
Somewhat important	2
Of minor importance	1
Not applicable; of no importance	0

PERFORMANCE RATING

Superior	9–10
Above average	7–8
Average	5–6
Below Average	3–4
Inferior	1–2

The rating system can also be used to evaluate the agency during the time it is serving the company. Many companies want to have semiannual reviews of agency performance so that the agency and the company can trade critiques on performance and service in an effort to eliminate potentially serious ruptures in their relationship.

The selection processes outlined here are not used by all clients. But the system does make it possible to carefully examine an agency, its people, and the way they link. If a company plans to spend between $100,000 and $1 million on outside counsel, the public relations manager would do well to use all or some of the elements discussed.

How much does a public relations counsel cost? The answer is that costs vary. They are based not only on the experience of the counseling firm but also on the amount of time that the firm expects to spend working for the company. Salary costs are always the starting point in developing fees.

Almost all agencies will tailor their method of charging for services to fit a specific corporate policy. However, the basis always will be the salary paid those expected to work on the business multiplied by a factor of 2½ or 3. The range of hourly charges and other agency costs are explained in the earlier chapter dealing with budgeting procedures.

After agreement has been reached on the method of compensation, the company and the agency become partners. As with any corporate task, the assignment will be difficult if the job is not defined. That may seem like a simple chore. The truth is that even after a long agency search, many companies still enter into a relationship with a counseling firm without defining the objectives they want the agency to achieve. Establish objectives, make them measurable to some degree, and insist that the public relations counsel use the four-step process of public relations: research, planning, execution, and evaluation.

Many professionals in counseling firms, like their counterparts in public relations departments, often ignore the research and the planning and go directly into the execution of projects. When this happens, they often become the executioner of public relations as a management function. Disciplined business managers in all other areas follow careful steps to achieve their objectives. In evaluating public relations, they anticipate the same type of careful step-by-step approach. When the research is not done or is done poorly, the plan and the execution may have little impact on a company's problem. Conversely, even with good research, a poor plan will doom the prospects for success.

The execution phase of public relations is the one most people see—this is the press release writing, the press conference staging, the media placements, the community leader seminars, the campus visits. Often it is not until this step in the process that agencies are called to work. This is probably one of the reasons that many corporate public relations managers express dissatisfaction with counseling. They do not involve the agency early enough in research and planning.

Evaluation of activities is nearly impossible unless a good plan has been prepared with measurable objectives established on the basis of sound research. Public relation managers often do not consider this when they talk about measuring effectiveness.

Should corporations have outside counsel? The answer is generally yes, but only if they understand that an agency can perform only as well as it is allowed to. If agencies are allowed to act as professional counselors, they will do so. If they are used only to fill in when the corporate public relations department staff cannot handle the work load, they won't produce the same results.

Further information on counseling can be obtained from the Counselors Section, Public Relations Society of America, 845 Third Avenue, New York, N.Y. 10022.

INDEX